RESPONSIBILITY AND MORALITY

RESPONSIBILITY AND MORALITY

HELPING CHILDREN BECOME RESPONSIBLE AND MORALLY MATURE

LARRY C. JENSEN
KAREN M. HUGHSTON

BRIGHAM YOUNG UNIVERSITY PRESS

Library of Congress Cataloging in Publication Data

Jensen, Larry C   1938—
    Responsibility and morality.

    Bibliography: p. 171
    1. Socialization. 2. Moral education. I. Hughs-
ton, Karen, joint author. II. Title.
HQ783.J46   301.15'72   79-10727
ISBN 0-8425-1679-4

BRIGHAM YOUNG UNIVERSITY PRESS

To Laury and Jani Sue

Contents

PART 1
THE
THEORY

1
GOALS

Many adults, committed to teaching moral values, are finding that their techniques are not working. Their children do not seem to be responding, to be behaving "the way they're supposed to." Some feel, further, that society does not encourage moral maturity in the young child. Instead, children learn concepts such as "Get all you can"; "Get what you want *now*"; "Stealing is O.K. as long as you're not caught"; "Take advantage of the other guy—it will help you get further ahead"; "Think of yourself first"; "Don't get too upset about violence, it happens all the time"; "If it feels good, do it." Similar undertones are often heard in popular media. Many adults fear that unless children are taught differently, these hedonistic philosophies will become their only values.

TRADITIONAL AND MODERN MODES OF TEACHING MORALITY

Today's diverse values have not always prevailed. During the last century a "simple" solution was popular. We will consider this solution under the heading of socialization.

In 1834 the Mother's Magazine *described a 16-month-old girl who refused to say "Dear Mama" upon the father's order. She was led into a room alone where she screamed wildly for ten minutes; then she was commanded again, and again refused. She was then whipped, and asked again. This was kept up for four hours until the child finally obeyed. (Sunley, 1968, p. 13.)*

Socialization

In describing nineteenth-century childhood training practices, Robert Sunley points out that obtaining obedience was the primary goal of socialization; it was accomplished by teaching the child to obey commands quickly and completely. Such training ordinarily began during the child's second year.

Although a gradual evolution toward moderation occurred in the nineteenth century, the general theme stressing obedience in the development of character traits continued throughout the century.

Obedience and Self-Growth

Today less stress is laid on conformity, and more concern is shown for the personal growth of a child. The individual's creating his own goals and gradually developing the ability to attain them have become more popular. Obedience to authority, tradition, or principles, while desirable, may not lead to maximum long-term self-growth. An example of this distinction between the goals of obedience and self-growth is illustrated in the findings from a large research project undertaken in the middle part of this century (Peck and Havighurst, 1962). Table One contains an outline of the basic types of moral characters identified in their study. The last two are of special interest because they illustrate that children are not to be evaluated in terms of their obedience and compliance. Obedience during childhood is not a sufficient indicator of overall psychological emotional growth and eventual adult maturity.

Goals for Children

When teachers and parents are asked what they want their children to be like, they usually respond: "I would like them to learn to behave, to be pleasant and happy, to be easy to get along with, to be able to make decisions, and to become a productive member of society." These are long-term goals, of course. A *short-range goal* can be accomplished "shortly," sometime during the next hour, day, or week. A *long-range goal* will not be accomplished, perhaps, until the child is an adult. However, long-term goals need to be set early in a child's life so that short-range goals can aim toward reaching them.

We have found, when working with parents of young children, that their long-range goals seem to be similar. They desire their children to be happy, likable, caring, independent, able to make decisions and direct their own behavior, to contribute to society, to be honest, hard-working, empathetic, and capable of making mature moral decisions.

Examining Goals

Keeping these long-range goals in mind, a parent or teacher can examine short-range goals to see if they will help the child achieve the long-range goals. Unfortunately, many teachers and parents are interested in the short-range goal of "getting the child to behave"; and though there are many techniques of achieving this goal, not all of them will help achieve the long-range goal of helping the child to become independent or able to make mature moral decisions. Through force or punishment children can be made to do almost anything, but can force guarantee internalization and later desired behavior? Research indicates it cannot.

If an adult insists on obtaining obedience, he will have to rely on disciplinary measures that require punishment—measures referred to as *high-power* techniques. The effectiveness of this kind of power in producing a more moral child has become suspect.

Power and Obedience

Consider the following incident. Thirty-five kindergarten boys were asked to rate five toys. Half the boys were promised in addition an attractive flashlight and the other half two so-so marbles. The boys were left alone with the toys but were told that if they played with their second-favorite toy, they would not receive the promised gift of a flashlight or two marbles.

As you might expect, the boys did not play with the forbidden second-favorite toy. But that was not the point of this experiment. What is interesting is that when the boys ranked the toys a second time, the rating of the second-favorite, forbidden toy was changed.

Those threatened with the loss of two marbles lowered the attractiveness of the forbidden toys, but the boys who were threatened with the loss of the flashlight now thought the forbidden toy was more attractive. They ranked it first. What is the lesson to be learned?

Using a more *powerful* incentive to deter or stop an action actually increases the desire to continue that action. A *mild* threat and the loss of two unimportant marbles eventually resulted in a lower motivation to play with the forbidden toy (Pepitone, McCanley, and Hammond, 1967).

A similar and even more interesting experiment has now been published (Leeper, 1973). Some children received a strong threat to keep them from playing with attractive toys, other children received a mild threat, and still other children received no threat at all.

Three weeks later the experimenter returned and asked all the children to play a game to obtain attractive prizes. The catch was this: only by falsifying their scores, being dishonest, could the children win a prize. The experimenter correctly predicted from his theory that subjects who received only a mild threat would falsify their scores the least, while those receiving a strong threat would be most dishonest. He reasoned that if the subjects did not play with the forbidden toys when receiving a mild threat, they considered themselves *good* boys. But

5

those who had received a strong threat would reason differently; they would conclude that they were *bad* boys because a strong threat was necessary to keep them from deviating.

These two experiments represent a score of similar experiments leading to at least one important principle, simply stated: *Use as little power as possible.*

The question of using power is probably the primary and most frequent question facing adults. Adults often underestimate just how much power they wield in dealing with young children.

ELEMENTS
CONTROLLED
BY PARENTS:

- Food and water
- Activities and opportunities
- Money and other socially attractive incentives
- Possession of information and knowledge
- Affection
- Love
- Pain
- Personal possessions (a car, clothing, playthings)

When adults use one or more of these elements to control or influence their children, they are using *high-power* techniques. Generally, that power can be classified into two divisions: reward and punishment. Ample research exists to show that both reward and punishment work. However, while punishment can be effective, it can also be damaging.

SOME
DISADVANTAGES
OF USING
PUNISHMENT:

- Punishment promotes negative feelings between the punished and the punisher.
- It often causes the punished to withdraw from the learning situation.
- It promotes sneakiness and deception to escape detection.
- It usually has only a temporary effect on behavior.
- It requires continued use, surveillance, and much energy.
- Adults eventually lose the ability to punish.
   Reliance on using rewards can also create problems.

SOME
DISADVANTAGES
OF USING
REWARDS:

- Children come to expect a payoff for their behavior.
- Children stop behaving when rewards stop, sometimes with a strong negative reaction.
- Parents lose ability to compete with other sources of reward, such as clubs, peers, and other desirable motivations.
- Children develop the feeling that external causes (the rewards) rather than internal elements control their actions.

Research indicates that if a parent wants to produce obedient children, high-power approaches are effective. If you want children who are compliant, obedient, submissive, courteous and proper—with the least effort in the shortest time—judiciously control and administer reward powers. Dispense rewards only when the child acts in a way you desire. In fact, it is almost impossible to avoid using high-reward power during the first two years when the children's communication skills are less developed and their comprehension is limited.

You might ask, "If high-reward power is so effective, why not use it?" You might add, "I'll settle for a child like that!" However, upon further reflection, you will likely conclude that you want more, that instead of *obedience* during childhood, you desire a higher goal. The higher goal is maturity.

This change in goals assists *low-power* techniques to succeed. Low-power techniques will better facilitate the development of personal growth. Although obedience during childhood may be compatible with personal growth toward maturity, in many cases quickly obtained obedience works against long-term growth. This may become apparent as we discuss low power. The emphasis on individual growth and the elements of low power need to be explained. First, what do adults do if they don't use high-power reward and punishment?

HOW TO FACILITATE A CHILD'S GROWTH TOWARD MATURITY

- Give love and affection.
- Talk, listen.
- Share feelings.
- Accept as much of a child's behavior as possible.
- Give trust to children even when you know they will not succeed at a given task.
- Provide information.
- Provide experiences and consequences.

Create an Atmosphere for Personal Growth

- Expect reasonable achievement.
- Expect logic and rationality.
- Expect a child to solve his or her problems. (To become independent.)
- Expect a child to be aware and considerate of other people's feelings.
- Expect a child to be informed about essentials of life.

Place Responsibility on the Child

Note that the first listings are actions for adults. However, the entire system would fail if the bottom list were absent. This list consists of actions expected of the child. When an adult uses low-power techniques, the child is an *active* participant.

She is not a passive person acted upon by powerful adults. She will not have to perform for rewards or receive punishments. Instead she will realize what is expected of her and will respond to an adult who not only trusts in her but who is also ready to help. The adult becomes a growth facilitator, a partner in growing, rather than a domineering authority who assumes the responsibility for the child's growth.

The primary advantage of low-power discipline is that it better prepares a child for independence that later comes with maturity. At age twenty-one children of low-power upbringing will be ahead in independence. It is probably true that when you use low power, children will not always come as promptly when you call them; they will not persist as long on a tiring, boring task; and they will make more mistakes in carrying out assignments. You will feel more frustration that you do not have as much control when you issue an order, and you may not receive as much respect. However, the responses you do receive from children when you use low-power techniques are likely more genuine and enduring, and it is given from love and real concern for your wishes. The motivation is different.

The real test is what children will be like when adults are no longer with them. A father who received respect from his young children by either threatening them with punishment or promising them large rewards will receive less respect when his children are grown than the father who used low-power techniques.

Often parents exclaim, "But he was such a good child, I don't understand how he could have turned out so bad." Likely, this child was being highly rewarded for his good behavior and punished for bad rather than being allowed to learn through experiencing freedom to make mistakes during childhood. He did not acquire controls from within because he was being controlled from without. When this outward control is removed, an individual lacks an internal personal guidance system that could have come from low-power disciplinary techniques. Such techniques provide opportunities for acquiring inner controls based on logic or rationality, awareness of feelings, and concern for others. Note not only the absence of coercion but also the necessity for providing a growth-promoting environment with standards, expectations, and values.

The instructional materials presented in this book were developed to help teachers and parents clarify long-range goals for children, specifically in the area of moral development. At the same time, the program presents short-range goals and techniques of achieving long-range goals. Often, obtaining desired moral behavior is somewhere "up in the clouds." We hope that through the techniques and problem-solving tasks presented in this book, ways of achieving desired moral behavior can be brought "down to earth."

Table 1: Behavioral Types

(Compiled from information taken from Peck and Havighurst, 1962, pp. 5–8.)

Amoral	This type of behavior corresponds to what is often called clinically the "psychopathic personality." Such a person follows his whims and impulses without regard for the way such actions affect other people. He considers himself the center of the universe and sees other people or objects as means to direct self-gratification.
Expedient	A person of this type is primarily self-centered and considers other people's welfare and reactions only in terms of gaining his personal ends. He tends to get what he wants with a minimum of giving in return. He behaves in ways his society defines as moral, only so long as it suits his purposes.
Conforming	This kind of person has one general, internalized principle: do what others do and be governed by what they say. He conforms to all the rules of his group. He wants to do what others do, and his only anxiety source is possible disapproval.
	The conformist is seen most often in stable folk societies. He learns, more by habit than by awareness of moral cause and effect, to behave in each specific situation in a certain prescribed way. He is kind and loyal to his family and tribe because he is rewarded for acting in one way, punished for acting another way.
Irrational-Conscientious	This is the person who judges a given act according to his own internal standard of right and wrong. In the adolescent or adult of this type, conformity to the group code is not the issue. Rather, it is conformity to a code he has

9

internalized and believes in. If he approves of an act he sees as honest, he carries it out whether or not the people around him approve. The irrational component is visible in the individual's customary rigidity in applying preconceived principles, somewhat in the manner of the conformist.

Rational-Altruistic	The rational-altruistic person has reached the highest level of moral maturity. Such a person not only has a stable set of moral principles by which he judges and directs his own action; he objectively assesses the result of an act in a given situation and approves it on the grounds of whether or not it serves others as well as himself. . . . He is "rational" because he assesses each new action and its effects realistically, in the light of internalized moral principles derived from social experience; and he is "altruistic" because he is ultimately interested in the welfare of others as well as himself.

2 UNDER-STANDING THE YOUNG CHILD

Parents often rationalize: "I just don't *understand why* he does those things when he knows better," or "I'll *never understand* him," or "Why can't he just do the things he knows he *should*," or "I won't worry about the behavior; it is just a *stage* of *development* he is going through." Teachers and parents are trying to understand why children do what they do and why they behave in negative ways when they have been "taught" better. This chapter will briefly discuss theories of how young children develop through stages and how the child's movement through these stages affects his or her moral reasoning behavior. The chapter will also discuss a child's emotional needs, how children learn, and how parents and teachers can retard or promote children's morality.

CHILDREN'S NEEDS

In considering how children learn, parents and teachers must ask: what should they learn, when and where should that learning take place? The answers to these questions will provide goals for children. Decide first what will help children enjoy life more fully, what will help them become productive members of society, and what will help them develop their fullest potentials.

Children never stop learning. The *when* of learning depends not only on the level of the children's development but also on the degree of the child's interest. Adults must realize that learning is a continual process; a child is learning something all the time. Teachers and parents need to plan carefully activities that support goals for children and that encourage maturity of moral thought.

In order to provide childhood experiences that will contribute to a child's development, an adult should be sensitive to the special needs of the child and should gain an understanding of the stages of development toward reaching maturity. The adult first must gain an understanding of *developmental tasks* necessary for each stage of development.

Basic to children's mental health are needs for *security, safety, belonging, recognition, approval, independence,* and *self-esteem.* The tasks necessary for developing these characteristics must be mastered if an adult is to maintain a desired course of development for a child.

Trust One of the most critical steps in human development is the development of trust—the first and most important step in acquiring maturity in moral thinking. Children who never develop trust have difficulty with all the other developmental tasks in later stages. A child who cannot feel trust for another person is not able to trust himself. Positive interactions with other individuals as well as feelings of self-worth are impaired when the child has not successfully completed this stage of development.

On the other hand, if completion of the stage is successful, this does not mean that the child will always feel trustful and that this trust cannot be destroyed by a hostile environment. But the trustful child will have an easier time coping under adverse conditions and will still continue to need love, encouragement, support, consistency, and respect. Hostility and ridicule in the classroom or in the home can destroy the level of trust a child had achieved at an earlier stage of development. Most psychologists conclude that affectionate and accepting relationships are necessary to foster a sense of security and healthy independence—prerequisites for optimum learning.

A Democratic Atmosphere A democratic atmosphere is conducive to learning because a child must learn to rely on his own thinking and reasoning without depending on an adult authority to "tell" him what is right and wrong. Many adults feel uncomfortable with this type of interaction because they have learned that the adult should at all times be the supreme authority. Ironically, few adults would ever admit to be "all-knowing," but many seem to give the impression they are. However, no adult can be "all-powerful," having total control of children at all times.

If parents and teachers would consider what it would be like if our government were based solely on the principle of power, they would more clearly understand how children feel when they are subjected to power-oriented control.

It is true that children have not had the experience and do not possess the abilities for making as mature decisions as many adults, but they will never learn unless they are given the opportunity. Children can be given many opportunities to do independent and critical thinking without an adult telling them they are right or wrong. How is this to be directly implemented?

Decision Making

As a child progresses through stages of development, he needs to be given not only guidance but also freedom, along with responsibility, to accomplish the developmental tasks within each stage. Giving him complete freedom, of course, would not only be irresponsible, it would be dangerous; the child needs to be protected from the natural hazards of life.

AUTONOMY

However, research has shown that in the stage of autonomy (toddler—ages one to 2½ years) a child is curious, sensory, active, and experimenting. Ideally, he should be allowed to play with the pots and pans and to use his senses in many different ways: tasting, seeing, feeling, hearing, and smelling. This is how a child learns. The child who is kept in the playpen most of the day does not achieve this sense of autonomy, the task that must be developed at this stage if he is to achieve the other stages. The child at this stage, however, lacks judgment and therefore needs to be watched constantly. Though he needs space, time, and freedom to explore, his freedom must be accompanied by limits.

A child must be respected and must learn respect for others' needs. Moral maturity becomes simply that—consideration of another's welfare as well as one's own. The young child is typically referred to as "egocentric," meaning that he is self-centered. This does not mean that he is selfish, but that he has not yet had enough experience to understand or appreciate someone else's point of view. He sees everything from his point of view and does not understand why others do not see it that way as well. The child at this stage realizes that his body is separate and different from other objects, including people, but he does not realize his experiences are his alone. He does not understand that his thoughts and actions make up only a part of the situation in which he participates. Because of this stage of egocentricity (which is the most apparent during toddlerhood and the preschool years), a young child has difficulty achieving

EGOCENTRICITY

13

maturity in moral thought because he is unable to understand someone else's point of view.

COGNITIVE
AND MORAL
DEVELOPMENT

Piaget, a Swiss psychologist, has developed one of the best known and respected theories of how children's cognitive and moral thought develops—in stages. Each stage prepares the child for the next stage, in that each new experience is understood and becomes meaningful to her on the basis of previous meaningful and successful experience. With each new experience, meaningful to her, she progresses to the next higher stage of development.

In examining the cognitive and moral stages of development as defined by Piaget, we can see similarities. Table two shows his stages of moral development.

Transition

Because this book is written for the adult caring for the preschool or the early school-age child, the stage of development we are most concerned with is the heteronomous stage. The six- or seven-year-old child is in a stage of transition, which means that his social experiences can have an effect upon his progress throughout this stage. Piaget's theory states that progress through the stages of both cognitive and moral development is invariant and irreversible—that every child will go through each stage and through each stage in order. The child's social experience can influence only the speed and ease with which he or she progresses through the stages. The implication is that though the stages are invariant and irreversible, significant people in a child's life can make a difference as to whether his or her progress through the stages will be retarded, accelerated, or normal.

Lawrence Kohlberg (1971), a psychologist who has done a great deal of research and writing in the field of moral development, has formulated what he calls a cognitive-developmental approach to moral reasoning. He follows the tradition of Jean Piaget, emphasizing the stages of Piaget's theory. In addition, he has elaborated on Piaget's thinking and has developed a more specific theory. Basically, Kohlberg's first three stages are similar to the heteronomous orientation, and the upper three stages are similar to Piaget's autonomous level. Stages one through three, for Kohlberg, range from conformity in order to avoid punishment, to satisfying oneself, to gaining approval of others; stages four through six range from conformity as obedience to formal law, to a moral-social contract involving the welfare of self and others, to a focus on higher principles of personal conscience. Note the similarity of Kohlberg's theory presented in table three to that of Peck and Havighurst (table one).

Kohlberg argues that once moral reasoning is developed, it will apply to a wide range of circumstances, not only the ones discussed. Obviously, this characteristic is important in a changing world in which future problems cannot always be anticipated, and a present and future society must place confidence in future leaders to solve and resolve difficult moral dilemmas.

The importance Piaget attaches to innate development is reflected in his use of the word *stages* and his implicit undertone that moral development is almost universal among children given the basic rudiments of social life. On the other hand, Piaget also emphasizes that social experiences have an effect on moral reasoning. (Boyce and Jensen, 1978.) *Social Experience*

Piaget has documented at least two primary elements influencing moral development. These are 1) the constraint of adult authority and 2) mutual peer respect. Piaget has skillfully systematized these two origins of moral thinking into a coherent theory that is not only internally consistent but also compatible with other theories of cognitive development and logical thinking.

Piaget, Kohlberg, and other researchers believe that social (peer) interaction or mutual peer respect is a more superior form of learning than simply learning to be obedient to adult authority. (Boyce and Jensen, 1978.) In social interaction children must solve problems among themselves; these experiences result in improved reasoning. Social interaction is a state in which all the participants are considered equal, and a child learns that his own ideas are as valuable and important as others. The child must learn to give and take and must learn that compromise is a necessary and acceptable way of solving problems. In this way he comes to learn that rules and standards are necessary and that he, individually, can play an active part in forming them. This learning can be accomplished in the classroom and in the family if adults will relate to children on a more equal basis. *Compromise*

From the perspective of internalization a child develops the realization that morality comes from within and that one's principles can therefore no longer be dictated by outside authority. They must be examined and fully internalized for their adoption to be justified. The individual who reaches this point *Moral Internalization*

15

is morally autonomous, or mature, and the main vehicle for his growth seems to be active social interaction.

Most children (as well as adults) could be made perfectly obedient if ample power, surveillance, and consistency were constantly and intelligently applied. Obviously, these conditions cannot be met in a natural environment. In situations where a child knows he is being observed, where the rewards for desired behavior are high and punishment is severe for inappropriate behavior, there are many model children. What happens to these children when the external controls are removed and surveillance is impossible is hard to predict with certainty; but as we have discussed, an internal motivation is preferable.

If children are observed to behave appropriately with few external controls, they will behave appropriately even when not being observed. When children do this, they are said to have internalized standards and values and to have motivation from within.

Internalized actions may be synonymous with what is often called conscience, wherein a person feels a moral obligation to abide by some behavior and experiences guilt when he does not. Some internalized behaviors are more related to a pleasure in doing the positive act, as in prosocial behaviors such as sharing, helping, and empathizing.

Martin Hoffman (1970) describes three levels of internalization. The most primitive is based on conditioned fear. For example, a child who is repeatedly punished for a particular behavior gradually becomes anxious when she thinks about the act. She learns to avoid the behavior and thereby dispels the anxiety. Although this process might be defined as internalization, since the child will behave morally in the absence of the punishing person, Hoffman feels that this can be only a borderline morality because the child is motivated solely by external threat, not by evaluating her behavior.

The second type of internalization occurs when an individual adopts standards out of respect for others. He believes in and abides by the standards not because of their content, but because they were given to him by individuals he respects.

When an individual views standards as worthwhile in and of themselves, she experiences the third level of internalization. She accepts the obligations of the rules as her own and acts to avoid self-condemnation, not the condemnation of others. More will be said about internalization in the next chapter.

As we have said, Piaget believed that moral maturity is developed through stages that are orderly, maturational, and in-

16

variant and that both maturation and experience play a role in the transition from one stage to the next. Kohlberg added that some forms of social participation are especially stimulating to moral development. Other forms that lack opportunities or arouse inhibiting anxieties retard progress through the moral stages and perhaps fix the individual permanently at an early stage.

Children's Play

In a comparison of the theories of Piaget, Erikson, and Kohlberg, the striking similarity is that there is movement from a focus on self to a focus on others. This movement, however, takes time and requires that the child first have his or her emotional needs filled and have many opportunities for social interaction with adults and children. This development can be understood by considering what we know about children's play. As a child moves through the *stages of play* and has opportunities to interact with other children, his ability for mature social interaction increases. The first stage is that of *solitary play,* which occurs during infancy and early toddlerhood, in which the child plays alone. The second stage is that of *parallel play,* which occurs during late toddlerhood and early preschool, in which the child enjoys the company of others but still basically plays alone; the child plays *beside* another child but not *with* him. Interactions, when they occur, tend to be rough and aggressive because the child has not yet learned to "take the role of the other." He is *egocentric* and cannot yet understand how another child feels when he takes a toy away or pushes the other child down. Other children are treated much the same way as toys are. Sometimes they are "hugged to pieces," and at other times they are pushed aside or completely ignored. The third and last stage of play is known as *cooperative play,* in which a child plays *with* another child. The play is organized and purposeful, and, most important, the child has learned to "give" as well as "take." He has now progressed to the point where he can understand that others have feelings and rights too. Although this stage has its beginnings in the preschool years, growth occurs each year until adulthood.

Summary

The ability to create, nourish, and fulfill others' needs is not an ability achieved overnight but one that develops over a period of years and one that can be developed only as a person achieves the various stages of development.

The first and most important stage focuses completely on fulfilling the needs of the "self." Children whose self needs are not fulfilled can never fully give to another person. On the oth-

17

er hand, children who have parents who *continue* to focus *only* on the child's *self* needs when he or she should be moving into a stage in which *other's* needs are becoming important will remain in the stage of egocentricity and will not be able to give to another person. So the balance is important.

Hopefully, parents and teachers, once familiar with the theories of the various stages, will know what is to be expected at each stage of development and will be better able to fulfill the child's needs at the appropriate time.

It is essential, however, that each child go through each stage. The social experience of each individual can retard or accelerate her or his movement through the stages. The next chapter will discuss how significant adults in a child's life can influence that child's development by the type of social experience he or she is encouraged to engage in, as well as by the type of discipline, communication, and general parent-child interactions that exist in the classroom.

Table 2: Piaget's Stages of Moral Development

Piaget has defined two stages of moral development a child must pass through before becoming able to make mature moral judgments. These stages encompass both respect for rules and a sense of justice.

Stage 1 HETERONOMY	Stage 2 AUTONOMY
• Subject to another's law • Dependent on adult authority • Obligation to comply to rules because they are sacred and unalterable • Unconditional respect • Egocentric • Behaviors viewed as "totally right or totally wrong"—inability to see the "grey," only the black and white • Thinks that others view behaviors in the same way as the child • Inability to focus on more than one dimension of an act (cannot attend to both consequences of an act as well as intentions at the same time. When there is a conflict such as a child falling and breaking another child's airplane, the consequences are focused on and the act is judged as "bad" or "naughty" when it was, in fact, an accident. The consequences are judged on rightness or wrongness, extent of conformity or established rules, and whether it elicits punishment)	• Ability to see things from another person's point of view • Appropriate timing—ages 6–8 • "Subject to another's law" • Stage of "cooperation or reciprocity" • Less dependent on adult authority for judgments • Child does not view rules as rigid or unchangeable but as established and maintained through reciprocal social agreement • Rules subject to modification in response to human needs or other situational demands • Judgments of rightness and wrongness no longer determined only by the consequences but also by intentionality • Now believes that punishment should be related to the misdeed • Stage comes about as a result of social interaction in which cooperation is an essential by-product

Table 3: Kohlberg's Stages of Moral Development

Lawrence Kohlberg (1963) has defined six developmental stages. These stages are ordered into three levels of motivation for morality.

Stage One: Premoral	Type 1.	Obedience because of punishment and fear
	Type 2.	Obedience to receive rewards for self
Stage Two: Morality through conformity	Type 3.	To receive approval from others, with no relationship to rules of right and wrong.
	Type 4.	To receive approval of an authoritative adult and to publicly adhere to explicit rules.
Stage Three: Mature morality	Type 5.	Based on agreements, contracts, and socially derived rules
	Type 6.	Based on conscience and principles. A rational person reacting to standards of truth, knowledge, and human dignity.

3
THE ROLE
OF THE
ADULT

"I just don't know what to do with him. Every day he goes to the corner grocery store and steals something—candy, gum, or crackers. Then he comes home, runs into his room, hides, and eats what he has stolen. We punish him and tell him that stealing is not right, but he keeps on doing it. He has been taught better. The thing that worries me most is that it is getting worse, and he thinks it's funny. He even laughs when we spank him. What will I ever do?"

The above is an example of one of a number of common problems that parents must deal with. A family counselor would probably ask this mother how *she* feels when the child steals the candy and how *she* feels when he laughs during the punishment. According to Alderian counseling, this child is misbehaving for a reason, and whatever that reason might be (to get attention, to rankle his mother, to hurt), the child's misbehavior continues because he is "getting something out of it." The parents are rewarding the misbehavior. (Dreikurs and Soltz, 1964.)

In the previous chapter moral maturity was defined as the ability to make decisions—based on an *internalized* feeling of what is right and wrong. A person who is morally mature makes decisions based not only on conformity or "the right thing to do," but on feelings of respect and care for other individuals. In other words, a morally mature person would avoid stealing not only because it is against the law or because most people think it is wrong but because stealing does not respect another person and will hurt the person who is robbed.

Children and adults, we believe, will come to think more maturely as they face and consider moral issues as problems.

Parents who allow their children an opportunity to face life's problems and who do not impose upon them pat, absolute decisions are fostering their ability to understand moral issues. For the growing mind the exact solution is not important. Instead it is the process or experience of *thinking* that produces moral maturity. Often the thinking is aided by information from another person. For the child this is usually a sibling, a peer, or a parent.

Peer Interaction vs. Adult Interaction

Piaget emphasizes the importance of social experience in the development of moral maturity. His focus is on peer interaction and the child's ability to learn to give and take in a social group. Piaget also states, however, that the child's environment does affect his progress through the stages of moral maturity. Similarly, adults in a child's life are a very important part of that child's environment. Though peer interaction is extremely important in the development of a child's sense of equality, justice, rules, cooperation, and respect, the parents, teachers, and other significant adults in a child's life are equally important in developing those qualities. Moral maturity results from interaction and cooperation with both adults and peers.

Parents—The Most Important Socializing Agent

What kind of interaction best facilitates the development of moral maturity? Many parents think that if they send (or take) their children to Sunday School, they will grow up to be morally mature. But Sunday School is not the important socializing agent in the development of moral maturity. Those people with whom children spend the greatest amount of time will have the deciding effect on their development.

Teachers a Help to Parents

Teachers also serve an important role. For example, a child who comes from a poor home in which the parents discourage moral maturity can learn to respond in a different way in the classroom because of a teacher. Sometimes a teacher throws up her hands and says, "I can't do a thing with this child. His parents are such poor models. How can I teach the child something that his parents 'unteach' him at home?" This teacher has given up on the child—perhaps too soon. Many adults can remember teachers of whom they were especially fond and who had special influence upon their lives. Teachers may underestimate their important role.

22

Parents who find a teacher not exhibiting those behaviors that encourage moral maturity need not give up, and, more important, should not criticize the teacher in front of the child. Because the child at this young age possesses a unilateral respect for adult authority, a conflict between two of the most important people in his life—a parent and a teacher—presents conflict for the child. Teachers and parents should try to share encouragement and positive support.

Let us return to a question asked earlier, "What kind of interaction best facilitates moral maturity?" When early school-age children (ages five through nine) were asked what qualities they think a "perfect school teacher" should have, the most frequently repeated qualities were as follows: nice, understanding, teaches you a lot, fair, helps you, listens, has a good attitude, doesn't get mad all the time, happy, considerate, knows kids, allows freedom in the classroom, helps us learn, lets us work on our own, and not a lot of homework. Nearly every child interviewed said that a "perfect" or "good" school teacher should be "nice," "teach a lot (in an easy way)," and "not get 'mad' or angry all the time."

From this survey and from other literature on teaching techniques and parental qualities helpful or not helpful in stimulating moral maturity, we have compiled the following lists. (See table four.)

Adults who care for and work with children might carefully examine this list of qualities and behaviors and check which behaviors are more typical of themselves. The task is not to see on which side of the list one has the *most* checks but to determine if there are checks on the side listing behaviors discouraging or inhibiting moral maturity. If there are, the adult should understand why moral maturity may be a problem for the child. In examining the side listing those behaviors encouraging to or stimulating moral maturity, the focus should not be on the *number* of checked behaviors but on those behaviors not checked. The adults should then determine what possible effect the lack of certain behaviors or characteristics will have on the moral maturity of the child.

The following section provides further explanation and emphasizes the value of some of the characteristics and behaviors that encourage or stimulate moral maturity.

Most behavioral scientists in psychology, pediatrics, psychiatry, and sociology have concluded that affectionate and accepting relationships are necessary to foster a sense of security and healthy independence—prerequisites for optimum learning. Affection brings feelings that express concern, warmth, regard, caring, sympathy, and helpfulness.

Children who are smothered with affection are not given opportunities often to express their own affections. This is often referred to as "smother love." The problem is that over-affection on the part of adults tends to fulfill the adult's needs and desires and not the children's. They should allow children to be active in giving as well as receiving.

LOVE Love is an emotion that often grows out of affection but is much stronger and more complex. Love involves a feeling of deep attachment and commitment. Healthy emotional development of a child is dependent upon adequate expressions of love. A classroom or home in which there is love helps children develop positive attitudes and behavior toward themselves, their family and friends, teachers, and society in general. A positive, supportive, and trusting relationship with an adult is needed especially in early infancy as well as throughout the child's life. Related to love is the development of *trust,* the first step to a healthy personality.

As we mentioned earlier, these two emotions, love and affection, stimulate feelings of security, trust, and healthy independence—prerequisites for learning and future moral maturity.

UNDERSTANDING
AND
COMMUNICATING
ACCEPTANCE
Like an adult, a child needs to know that others understand her, that they will *listen* and try to put themselves in her place. This ability to put oneself in the place of another is called *empathy,* or the ability to take the role of another and try to understand how he feels.

How is acceptance communicated? If a child is working on a task, is making obvious and numerous mistakes, and the parent says, "Let me show you how to do it," this is a subtle form of rejection. Let the child complete the task; nonintervention is a sign of acceptance, a sign of confidence.

Another method is passive listening. If a child knows that an adult is really listening, that adult is conveying acceptance to the child. Note that in passive listening the adult does not really contribute anything to the conversation. He simply lets the child know that someone is interested in him.

Next is active listening, which begins when a child has a problem. The child takes a problem, puts it into words, and sends it to the parent. The parent decodes the message. Now the parent encodes the message, using other words, and sends it back to the child. For example, when the child sends the message: "When do we go home?" he may be trying to express that he is sleepy. The parent receives the message and decodes it thus, "The child wants to go to sleep." The parent then encodes the message and returns it by saying, "You're getting bored and sleepy in this place." The child then knows he is understood. In returning the message the parent ordinarily uses different words.

What results from active listening? First, it provides a child with a catharsis, an opening up and getting the feelings out, and it helps the child to become less afraid of feelings. It also promotes understanding between the child and the parent. Furthermore, active listening develops a problem-solving skill for the child. He still has the problem, and he must deal with it. Eventually the child will be more likely to listen to the parent's thoughts and ideas. Children tend to code thoughts and ideas and send messages to people who will listen. Active listening helps the child to think about the problem, solve it, and *handle it himself.*

Some common mistakes are made when active listening is used. One mistake is using active listening with the intent of manipulating the child and calling it guidance. The words "active listening" mean to send the message back and let the child solve his own problem. If a parent changes the message so that it solves the problem for the child, it is not active listening.

Parents can fall into the habit of parroting a child's statements. This occurs when the child sends a message; the parent does not recode the message but uses the same words the child used. The child soon realizes what the parent is doing and often feels that "Polly the parrot" would be equally warm and helpful. The child says, "Boy, I'm tired." And the parent says, "You're tired." The child does not know if the parent really understands. Accurate listening and coding can occur but will still fail if there is little real concern or caring communicated.

In summary, three techniques can be used when the child needs to solve a problem: (1) noninterference, (2) passive listening, and (3) active listening. (See Gordon, 1970.)

RESPECT

Respect is the foundation of moral maturity; at a very young age children need to know they are respected as persons. It is difficult for a young child to learn to respect adults when adults do not show respect for the child. Often we see what seems to be respect from a child who fears punishment by the adult. But fear is not respect and often is not maintained when the fear object (the adult) is not around. Achieving moral maturity requires that the child internalize morally mature behavior. When there is a lack of respect on the part of either the

25

adult or the child, mature moral internalization is seldom the result. One of the problems in our society is that too many adults are training children to disrespect the rights of others. One of the best ways for adults to help children respect the rights of others is to first respect themselves, then others, including the child. When an adult does not respect himself and allows children to use him like a door mat—manipulating him into doing everything for the child, the result is detrimental to both the child and the adult.

ENCOURAGEMENT   According to Rudolf Dreikurs (1964), "Encouragement is more important than any other aspect of child-raising. It is so important that the lack of it can be considered the *basic* cause of misbehavior. *A misbehaving child is a discouraged child.* Each child needs continuous encouragement just as a plant needs water. He cannot grow and develop and gain a sense of belonging without encouragement."

What is encouragement? According to Dreikurs, it is a "continuous process aimed at giving the child a sense of self-respect and a sense of accomplishment." Through encouragement the child is able to see that he is a capable and worthwhile person who is able to make decisions and direct his own behavior. This is not to say that the adults in a child's life cannot be of assistance; of course they can and should. Many parents and teachers, however, feel that being a "good parent" or a "good teacher" means to do as much as possible for the child. But by doing for the child what he can do for himself, the adult is telling the child that he is incapable. Teaching children is a task requiring good timing. Helping the child become independent does not mean completely turning over a task to a child who is not developmentally prepared to handle the task. Teaching must be done in small steps, but how those small steps are handled is what may make the difference in whether the child feels encouraged or discouraged, independent or dependent, worthwhile or not worthwhile.

Such statements as "You can do it," "I'm proud of you. Just one more piece and your puzzle will be complete." "You have done it all by yourself," help a child feel worthwhile, as though he could tackle a new task successfully. The adult is there for support and help, but the child is encouraged to do the task by himself. The often-heard statements of a young child, "I *can do* it all by myself" or "I *did* it all by myself" are examples of the young child's yearning to become independent and gain esteem from those who are important in his life.

26

In order to make mature moral decisions, an individual must maintain some level of independence as well as self-esteem, or a positive self-concept. A child who has been over-protected, over-indulged, humiliated, told (perhaps not in words) he is a failure, he has to be perfect, he is not needed, told over and over again that he is too small, too dumb, too young, too old, too clumsy, too stupid, too much trouble, too lazy, too fat or thin or whatever—such a child will not be able to make mature moral decisions. He has not been shown respect and cannot therefore make decisions based on respect for someone else. Because of his discouragement and perhaps his level of hurt, he may strike out or hurt back in a number of different ways, such as lying or stealing, or having always to be first, or wanting all the candy for himself, or not being able to resist temptation, or any number of morally immature acts. The child who does not receive encouragement from the significant adults in his life will not feel good about himself and will not have the courage to handle new challenges. Instead he will try to find the place he "belongs" in some way. The child will find it extremely difficult to give to another person because he has not been given to in the way he needs.

Half of the job of encouraging a child lies in avoiding discouragement either by humiliation or by over-protection. Anything we do that supports a child's lack of faith in himself is discouraging. The other half lies in knowing how to encourage. Whenever we act to support the child in a courageous and confident self-concept, we offer encouragement. There is no pat answer to the problem. It involves careful study and thought on the part of the parents [and teachers]. We must observe the result of our training program and repeatedly ask ourselves, "What is this method doing to my child's self-concept?"

The child's behavior gives the clue to his self-esteem. The child who doubts his own ability and his own value will demonstrate it through his deficiencies. He no longer seeks to belong through usefulness, participation, and contributions. In his discouragement he turns to useless and provocative behavior. Convinced that he is inadequate and cannot contribute, he determines that at least he will be noticed, one way or another. To be spanked is better than to be ignored. And there is some distinction in being known as "the bad boy." Such a child has become convinced that there is no hope of gaining a place through cooperative behavior. (Dreikurs, 1964.)

WHAT ADULTS SHOULD ENCOURAGE. In what ways should parents and teachers encourage children? In what should they be encouraged? First, children should be encouraged to think and act independently. Many adults encourage dependency. And though a certain amount of dependency is desirable, too much

27

interferes with the development: physical development, mental development, social development, and emotional development.

Courage. Adults and teachers should help their children to be courageous, not afraid to try new things. Children who have courage usually are more creative than those who fear failure or hold back.

Achievement. Children should be encouraged but not pressured to achieve. Adults who place unreasonably high expectations on their children set them up for failure and discouragement. Often children simply give up when they see that they cannot reach the high expectations set for them.

Independence. Children like to be encouraged to think independently. Adults can encourage independent thinking by asking the child for his or her opinion instead of always "telling" the child what is right or wrong. Adults can respond to children's answers by saying, "Good thinking," or "You have such good ideas. Can you think of another idea?" instead of saying, "That's wrong," or "That's not a good idea," or "Maybe somebody else has a better idea." Children who have been told that they are "good thinkers" or have "interesting or good ideas" begin to believe that they do and will continue to think creatively whether their answers are right or wrong.

Asking children questions requiring thought and reasoning rather than a simple yes or no helps stimulate thinking, and helping stimulate children's thought is an important teaching technique. It will assist children to become morally mature. The young child typically sees things as black or white or right or wrong. When the child is given a story with a moral conflict and is asked to consider the right thing for the character in the story to do, the child must do some critical and independent thinking.

Social Interaction. Children desire and need to engage in social interaction with children of their own age. Adults can help the child adjust to this relationship and progress in moral maturity by the way they encourage independence and problem solving among the social groups. For example, if a group of children are having an argument and the teacher or parent tries to solve the argument or to take sides, moral maturity is not encouraged, since the children are not trying to solve their own problems. Taking sides always causes conflict, since the adult never knows who started the argument or the fight. The adult can function as a mediator to help the children try to discover a solution to the disagreement by discussing the issue. The adult may say something like this, "It looks as if you two are having a hard time getting along today. Can you tell me about your problem?" One of the children tells the problem. The adult might respond with "I wonder if there is some way both of you can play with the truck at the same time so you can both be happy?" A child responds. The teacher states another idea: "Can you think of another idea that would make both of you happy?" The children cannot come up with a solution, so the adult must set a limit, still treating the problem as a group problem rather than one child's problem. The adult says, "I'm sorry you can't think of a way you can both use the truck today and be happy. I'll put the truck away, and maybe we can try again tomorrow."

This example is a typical sharing problem. Both children want the truck. They are unwilling to play with it together. They are unwilling to take turns. They are unwilling to do anything that would consider the other child's feelings; so the adult must set a limit and let the children try to work the problem out again at another time. The adult did not take sides, scold, or tell the children what they should do. Knowing this is a characteristic of the child at this young age, the adult turned over the responsibility of solving the problem to the children—with one limitation—that both sides be considered, and the solution must be fair to both sides. The children were unwilling to consider each other's point of view; so the teacher had to act in a way that wouldn't be unfair to either child. Perhaps the children will be more willing to cooperate or consider another person's point of view if they see that it will also benefit them.

Children, as mentioned before, are still egocentric when they start school and most often consider their own needs and desires before they consider someone else's. Expecting a young child to consider another person before himself is somewhat unrealistic, though it often happens. The more experience a child has in interacting socially with children his own age, the easier it will be for him to consider the other child's point of view. Adults can help or hinder this progression by the way they interact with the social group. Insisting on their sharing, or taking sides in arguments can hinder the progress of the child. Encourage the child (but do not force him) to consider the other person's point of view. Understanding he can't always have everything his way, that others have feelings too, that alternatives and solutions to problems can make more than one person happy, and that there are limits all of us must abide by are skills a young child must acquire for more mature moral decision making.

29

MODEL   An extremely important and powerful tool in teaching moral maturity is the model, or example, the adult sets for children. How many times have parents heard children say, "But *you* do it, Mommy." Most people believe, and studies substantiate, that children "listen" more to the example an adult sets than to what the adult says.

Children hear their parents say, "You shouldn't steal or be dishonest," then observe their parents picking up and eating a grape from the fruit counter or telling the ticket salesperson at the movie theater that her thirteen-year-old son is younger in order to pay a child's price for a movie ticket. What do children listen to? Do they learn that stealing and being dishonest is wrong at *all* times or do they learn from their parent's example that stealing and being dishonest is O.K. some of the time?

Parents often tell children not to fight with each other; then the parents fight. What do the children listen to? What the parents *do* or what they *say*?

Teachers who *tell* children they must be kind to all the children and not exclude anyone from their group, then have favorites in the classroom are not modeling the behavior they expect the children to exhibit. Often forgotten is the power of example; adults need to be careful to model those behaviors they want their children to exhibit.

DEMOCRACY   Democracy, to most of us, means freedom and equality. This is also true when we use the term democracy in dealing with children. In a classroom or home where a democratic atmosphere exists, a climate conducive to learning and to the development of moral maturity also exists.

Many adults feel unsure of the meaning of democracy. To some adults freedom means license, and equality means the loss of their "superior" status that allows them to dominate children and tell them what they can and cannot do.

In relation to the development of moral maturity, freedom does not mean license, but implies responsibility. We are free to do what we want only as long as what we do doesn't interfere with someone else's freedom. Respect for the freedom of others is paramount. For everyone to have freedom, order must exist, and order implies certain restrictions and obligations. A democratic atmosphere does not give children freedom to do whatever they want; that would encourage moral immaturity rather than maturity.

Equality implies that each individual has an equal right to dignity and respect. It is not realistic to think, however, that all

30

people are equal. We all have different abilities and different backgrounds and opportunities. But children need to learn that if a child in their classroom talks with a speech defect, for example, that child has an equal claim to dignity and respect. As children learn this principle from those important models in his life, he will progress morally.

Often those who disagree with the democratic method of dealing with children argue that freedom implies license. But adults who use democratic methods of working with children realize that children need limits and that without limits they do not really understand freedom and democracy. Using firmness in letting a child know how far he or she can go is very different from dominance. Dominance implies that the dominant person is superior and is always right. Many adults feel comfortable in the dominant, superior-inferior role, but this role is detrimental to the development of moral maturity.

FIRMNESS WITHOUT DOMINANCE

Sometimes a genuine conflict exists between the needs of the child and the needs of the adult. What should be done when these conflicts exist? The adult and the child can work together, using the following six steps:

USING A DEMOCRATIC PROBLEM-SOLVING DISCUSSION APPROACH

1. Identify and define the conflict.
2. Mutually generate possible alternative solutions. Do not try to decide initially the best solution, but attempt to get as many solutions out as possible.
3. Evaluate the alternative solutions.
4. Decide which is the best solution or the best *acceptable* solution.
5. Work out a way to implement the solution. How can it be put into practice?
6. Follow up and evaluate how this solution works.

Recognize that the solution may not be the best. If necessary, try it out; if it doesn't work, admit it is of poor quality. The children may communicate they do not like it. If so, begin again. Life then becomes a process of mutual problem solving between adult and child, effective because the child is motivated to carry out the solution. More chance exists of finding a high quality solution, and children develop thinking skills with less hostility. Furthermore, less enforcement or policing will be required, eliminating the need for power. The real problem is exposed, and children become more mature because they are treated like adults.

After making a decision, do not build in penalties for non-compliance. If penalties are to be imposed, they should be applicable to both parent and child. If possible, penalties and punishments for noncompliance should be eliminated. When agreements acceptable to all parties are broken, the approach should be "Let's take a look and see why this happened." A genuine agreement should be such that its implementation is desired by both parties. If problems develop, instead of using punishments and penalties, go back and set up a new agreement.

Confrontation   In some conflict situations, the teacher or parent must clearly and accurately present his or her beliefs and position to the child. This is done best with neither demands nor solutions, so that the child can share the problem common to both the adult and the child. With information plus communication from the adult, the child will have a problem on which he can focus. If it is in the realm of his own personal interest, he will likely present a resolution to the conflict. Frequently the resolution will be a compromise between his position and the adult's. If it is not a compromise or a concession but is opposed to the wishes of the adult, at this point the other factors discussed earlier might be considered: trusting, giving of freedom, or using the problem-solving approach. The solution should be judged in terms of whether it is growth-producing for one or for both of the participants.

Demands   Teachers and parents would be wise to extend only those demands that children are able to meet. In most cases development of the demand should come out of the communication between the child and the adult, rather than as an arbitrary decision by the adult. Ginott (1965) presents a dialogue that helps clarify a growth-promoting demand situation.

When a child is about to throw a stone at sister, mother should say, "Not at her, at the tree!" She will do well to deflect the child by pointing in the direction of the tree. She can then get at the feelings and suggest some harmless ways of expressing them:
"You may be as angry as you want at Sis."
"You may be furious. Inside yourself, you may hate her, but there will be no hurting."
"If you want to, you can throw stones at the tree and pretend it's your sister."
"If you want to, you can even draw her face on paper, stick it on the tree, and then throw stones; but she is not to be hurt."

Limits are accepted more willingly when they point out the function of an object: "The chair is for sitting, not for standing" is better than "Don't stand on the chair." "The blocks are for playing, not for throwing" is better than either "Don't throw blocks" or, "I am sorry I can't let you throw blocks, it is too dangerous." (pp. 119–120.)

Parents can take an active role in facilitating growth as described above—growth that can be seen in the circular nature of the child's environmental interaction. In general terms, the child who is inadequate meets his environment with decreased ability, increasing his chances of failure. The failure then reinforces or further strengthens his perception of himself as inadequate. Thus, a vicious cycle is set up, producing a lower self-concept.

The opposite is true for a healthy person. His success promotes subsequent feelings of adequacy. When a child is identified with others with a positive self-concept, he is most likely to meet them in an appropriate and successful manner, encouraging others to respond to him positively. He is then more likely to be able to identify with other people, having had successful experiences. Thus, success feeds upon success, and the process of growing towards self-fulfillment becomes self-perpetuating.

Process of Growth

If the preceding discussion seems too idealistic and impossible to achieve, a parent or teacher might take some comfort in the following:

First, most mistakes occurring in youth are not serious and can be reversed without serious consequences—if the mistakes do not constitute the total atmosphere. Childhood is the best time to make mistakes, but adults should remember that the day-to-day atmosphere and attitude in the home and in the school seem to be of more influence than occasional mistakes made by significant adults in a child's life.

Second, most parents do not learn to wait. A child must agree or comply immediately. What is the harm if a child says, "I won't," and after an hour or two of reflection says, "Okay, I will, you're right." Furthermore, when less pressure is used, an adult is more likely to hear this second statement from the child.

Last, adults can take comfort in knowing their children will likely grow toward psychological health despite parental errors. Change is inevitable. Teachers and parents can influence the

Final Statement

33

course of events in a child's life only to a degree. A parent, knowing that one is not totally responsible for a child's psychological growth, may learn to relax and relate with the child on a more equalitarian basis—to view the child as an already fully existing person and as a fellow human seeking self-fulfillment.

Table 4: Adult Behaviors Discouraging or Stimulating to Moral Maturity in Children

Discouraging Behaviors	Encouraging Behaviors
cold	showing affection
punishing	showing acceptance
rejecting	encouraging autonomy
hostile	encouraging courage
rigid	encouraging achievement
belittling	encouraging social interaction
critical	reinforcing good habits
unaccepting	stimulating ideas
neglecting	Knowledgeable about stages
authoritarian	of developmental needs
nagging	listening reflectively
overprotective	understanding
over-indulgent	fair
rewarding of fearful behavior	relaxed
suspicious	democratic
paying attention to immature	supporting
behavior	having a positive self-concept
discouraging independence	respecting self and others
encouraging extreme	giving of self freely
conformity	stimulating critical thinking
lacking a positive self-concept	noncritical
controlling	minimizing mistakes
	spending time training and
	teaching
	active (doesn't just talk)
	firm (without dominating)
	consistent (a child knows what
	to expect)
	modeling positive expected
	behavior
	separating the child from the
	punishment
	teaching skillfully
	modeling moral maturity
	happy
	considerate
	patient
	trusting
	loving

4
TEACHING
BASICS

Often a teacher or parent says, "I tried what that book said—'hog wash'! The only thing that happened is that the child got worse! I'm going back to my own techniques!"

Children are individuals, and techniques that work for one child may not work in the same way for another. An important but often neglected prerequisite is that the adult using the suggested techniques consider and examine the *principles of development* on which the suggested *techniques* are based. In other words, it is extremely important that adults have a firm knowledge and understanding of the principles upon which techniques arc based. Chapters two and three of this book discussed some principles of learning and of emotional, intellectual, and moral development, as well as principles involved in encouraging children's moral maturity. The more specific techniques discussed in this chapter are based upon these principles.

Without a firm knowledge and understanding of the principles governing the growth, development, and behavior of a child, an adult is at a loss when a technique doesn't work, as the example above illustrates. What then can one do when the techniques do not work? Listed below are some possible reasons for their lack of success.

- *Not enough time* has been put into applying the technique. Behavioral changes take time and consistency on the part of an adult working with a child. Behavior does not change overnight.

- A *lack of understanding* exists on the part of the adult as to why the technique is being used. This lack of understanding stems from an inadequate knowledge of the principles of child development.

- An adult *reinforces inappropriate responses.* Often adults do not realize they reinforce or reward (verbally and physically) behavior they do not want a child to engage in. A behaviorist would say that "if a behavior continues to be exhibited, it is being reinforced." Perhaps adults should look at whether they are reinforcing inappropriate responses.
- A *lack of or too much challenge* for a child. The child's ability to accommodate new information is limited, but if the information is too familiar or not challenging, he or she will not respond. In moral development the child cannot process information in more than one stage at a time. Studies (Boyce and Jensen, 1978) have shown that challenging a child's moral judgments with moral arguments one stage above the child's level is an effective way of raising the child's level, but arguments either too far above the child's level or too far below have little effect on him.

  An adult, then, needs to understand the developmental level of a child and, through interaction, evaluate his or her stage of moral development. The adult can then determine what kind of information or response would challenge the child to move to a higher stage of development.
- An *authoritarian* personality can promote failure. Often an adult tries very hard to allow a child to make decisions, and attempts to use democratic techniques. But the adult still maintains an air of authoritarianism that invokes fear or hostility in the child. Be aware of the tone of your voice and of nonverbal behavior, such as gestures and facial expressions.

  Often parents and teachers become nervous when they try to change authoritarian behavior. They fear the child will "run wild" and will be completely out of hand if they do not exert power. This is not true. As we discussed in an earlier chapter, democracy denotes respect both on the part of the child and on the part of the adult—respect prompted not by fear but by feelings of caring and understanding.
- *Permissiveness* on the part of the adult will not result in success. Adults often do not demand or expect respect from the child and thus do not follow through with any technique. Consider the following true example: A child and his mother in a large department store were waiting in line at the mail order desk. The child took a grocery cart in which the mother had placed her packages and pushed it back and forth over the feet of the woman standing next to them. The child's mother said sweetly with a smile on her face, "Now you mustn't run the cart over the poor woman's feet. That

hurts, and she doesn't like it. It's not nice to hurt someone's feet" (explaining, calling attention to the feelings of another person, setting limits). The words the mother used were appropriate; however, she did not follow through by enforcing the limits, and the child simply smiled at her and continued what he was doing. The mother ignored the situation, and the child finally stopped when the lady whose feet had been "mutilated" left and went to another part of the store. What did the child learn from this incident? A guess would be that he learned it is really okay to run over people's feet even though his mother had verbally said it wasn't okay. Mother's nonverbal behavior told the child the behavior was acceptable. What mother was really doing in this instance was reinforcing the child's misbehavior, teaching him *not* to be sensitive to the needs of others and not to listen to what mother says because she doesn't really mean it. Teachers often get caught in the same web of permissiveness.

The answer to what the mother in the above example "should" have done not only to stop the behavior but to encourage moral maturity does not lie in authoritarian techniques. Readers might respond with, "I would spank the child if he were mine," or "I would tell him if he doesn't quit it, he will have to go sit in the car," or "I would tell him if he would quit it, I would buy him an ice cream cone on the way home," or "I would jerk him away and make him go sit alone until I finished my shopping." Hopefully, the reader can see the futility of these solutions. Yet parents resort to these techniques day after day, partly out of ignorance and partly out of desperation. The behavior needs to be stopped immediately. What can be done? All of the above solutions would inhibit moral maturity and encourage moral immaturity. The very lowest stage of moral development, according to Kohlberg, is that in which a child chooses "right" to avoid punishment. The second stage is that in which a child chooses right to procure a reward.

The development of moral maturity involves responding to the needs of others. What the mother said in the first place was appropriate, but she did not follow through with actions. When the child continued to push the cart across the woman's feet, the mother should have said, "I can see that you are not able to handle the cart without bothering other people. I will have to push the cart myself. Next time we come, you can try again to handle the cart without bothering other people. Would you like it if someone pushed the cart across your feet?" The mother in this case pointed out the needs of another person, explained to the child the effect of his behavior, set limits, and followed through. Following through with established limits is an extremely important requirement in using any technique. There are occasions, however, when adults are wrong and can explain to the child that sometimes they make mistakes. Following through when you know you are wrong is not necessary to maintain an image or to encourage moral maturity. Children can accept that adults make mistakes. In fact, realizing adults can make mistakes can help a child progress toward moral maturity, in that a child is learning to see things as not always "black" or "white," and his thinking is becoming more flexible, less rigid. It is important, however, that the adult carefully consider what he or she expects of the child so that more often than not the adult is consistent.

Now that we have discussed some of the reasons why techniques in a book often do *not* work for adults, let us look at a few techniques that are the most effective in stimulating moral maturity in a child.

BE POSITIVE AND PREDICTABLE
Children tend to view the world as do the adults around them. If the adult is negative and constantly tells the child what he *can't do* rather than what he *can* do, the child begins to see the world as an unhappy and negative place. Everything is "out of bounds" for this child, and his response will be negative as well. An adult who is positive is one who sees the world as a happy place—and enjoys the children he or she works with. A positive adult is predictable. The child can count on his or her behavior being fairly consistent with environmental influences. Sometimes a child never knows whether other people are going to be happy or sad, pleasant or angry, hostile or relaxed. Unpredictable adult behavior produces a tense environment. The child has mixed emotions, sometimes feeling that an adult loves and cares for him, at other times feeling the adult hates him. A child subjected to this confusion day after day has a difficult time dealing with guilt feelings and often develops an overly sensitive or an inhibiting conscience. That little girl often develops emotional problems that can reduce her chance for understanding and having empathy for others. That little boy's development of a positive self-concept will undoubtedly be affected, and he may go through life trying to prove in one way or another that he is a worthwhile individual. In these instances, moral decisions are not based upon care and concern for the other person but on "how others see me" or on fear or rejection or punishment. Because a child's self-concept is suffering, he or she has difficulty seeing beyond his or her own needs or desires.

40

Teachers who have children in the classroom who come from homes where parents demonstrate unpredictable behavior can have a great effect on the children's moral development. By accepting a child, by showing him love, understanding, and compassion, by being predictable in his or her responses towards the child, a teacher can fill a most important role by helping that child regain trust in adults. This does not mean that the teacher must unconditionally accept everything the child *does*; the child, however, needs to feel that he is a worthwhile person. He needs to know that what *he does* can influence the behavior of adults around him. When he acts negatively, he can *predict* that his teacher will not be happy with him and will not respond positively. On the other hand, when he acts positively, he can *predict* that the teacher's response in most cases will be positive. He will be able to *communicate* with the teacher, and in those few cases where the teacher's behavior is *not* predictable, the child and the teacher can talk about it and discover why. Other environmental influences can affect the behavior of adults: lack of sleep, illness, or personal problems. In helping a child develop moral maturity, an adult must consider talking about these problems with a child. This will help the child develop empathy and understanding for others' problems.

Again, focus on the positive and on what the child is capable of rather than on what he cannot do. The overall objective of this technique is to *build the child's positive self-concept,* which will influence his ability to make mature moral decisions. Children who have a low self-concept often make decisions based on fulfilling their own needs or desires or counter-hurting another individual.

MINIMIZE MISTAKES

Many people falsely believe that if a child is accepted as he is, he will stay that way and will not improve. Parents also fear that if they accept their children's present behavior, their growth will be stifled. Parents also believe they can goad their children into further achievement and higher attainment by being unaccepting. The opposite is usually true. When a child feels accepted, and his mistakes are minimized, he will be free to grow, to change, to develop. But when he is heavily criticized, he stops changing because he now has to become defensive and protect himself. By being accepting, a parent will produce more change than by being nonaccepting.

However, *words* of acceptance are not enough. The parent and the teacher must demonstrate acceptance through *actions* so that a child *feels* the emotion. Obviously, it is unreasonable to expect parents to accept all a child's behavior, both acceptable and unacceptable. For example, destruction of property and aggression towards the helpless is unacceptable behavior. However, effective parents are said to accept more of their children's behavior than ineffective parents.

Teachers should move toward being as accepting as possible despite differences in children. One child may be extremely active and energetic; another may be quiet and may find his interest in books and music.

LISTEN TO CHILDREN

In order to facilitate the growth of character in children, adults must initiate effective communication, including sensitivity and listening. Sensitivity implies that listening is more than just hearing words; it also includes paying attention to such cues as nervousness, stuttering, facial expression, and loss of temper. An excellent example of listening is found in *Between Parent and Child* (Ginott, 1965):

When a child says: "I am not good in arithmetic," it is little help to tell him, "you are pretty lousy with figures," nor is it helpful to dispute his opinion or to offer him cheap advice. "If you studied more, you'd be better." Such hasty help only hurts his self-respect and the lesson decreases his confidence. His statement, "I am not good in arithmetic," can be met with earnestness and understanding. Any of the following would do: "Arithmetic is not an easy subject matter." "Some of the problems are very hard to figure out." "The teacher does not make it easier with his criticism." "He makes you feel stupid." "I bet you can't wait for the hour to pass" (p. 32).

Communication begins by listening to the other person without evaluating, trying to see things from his point of view. In most cases, if one genuinely listens and is sensitive to what the child has to say, he will find the child will have resources to cope with the problem and solve it. Perhaps presenting possible solutions would be called for as an intermediate process, but rarely is it helpful to dictate solutions at the outset.

Often children (and adults) do not understand how they feel or why they are saying what they are saying. When an understanding and *listening* adult can respond by reflecting back what a child is trying to say, that child can be helped to better understand his feelings and thoughts. Consider the following example: Randy came home from school one day, quite upset. He walked past Mother, past the refrigerator, past the bathroom, and straight to his room. He shut the door and locked it. Mother knew something was wrong and felt that if Randy could express his feelings, he might be able to better understand them, so Mother knocked on the door. "Randy, could I come in and put some clean socks in your drawer?" Mother entered the room and saw Randy stretched out face down on his bed with his head buried in his pillow. As Mother was putting away the socks she tried to reflect the feeling that she was picking up from Randy. "So you had a bad day at school today?"

Randy responded with, "Yep." Again mother tried to get Randy to talk. "Things didn't go so well." Randy exploded, "That dumb teacher of ours. She said the whole class will have to stay in fourth grade next year."

Mother responded with another reflection, "So your whole class will have to stay in fourth grade next year."

Randy continued, "Yeh, and we didn't do one thing."

Mother reflected, "Your class didn't do anything to make the teacher tell you you would have to stay in fourth grade next year."

Randy corrected, "Well, we did throw a few spit balls."

Mother responded nonjudgmentally, "You threw a few spitballs. That probably made the teacher mad."

"Yeah, it sure did. But she didn't have to get so mad at us. We were just having a little fun," Randy explained.

At this point, Mother could see that Randy was feeling much better and was getting a grip on how he felt. As the conversation progressed, with Mother not making any judgments or doing any nagging or "I told you so's," Randy finally was able to see the teacher's point of view and that the teacher had responded with a threat she later admitted she could not and would not follow through with. Because this mother listened and helped the child to understand his feelings, he was led to understand the feelings of others and to see the problem from someone else's point of view. Had the mother scolded, belittled, nagged, moralized, punished, or pried, the moral growth of her son would not have been encouraged. Listening is a very important technique in stimulating moral maturity.

Parents who tell children, "Do as I say, not as I do" are not setting a good model for children to follow. The children will more likely pay attention to what the adult *does* rather than what he *says*. Modeling, or the power of example, is possibly one of the most important and powerful tools an adult can use to help a child achieve moral maturity. As we have mentioned, inconsistency in word and deed can be extremely confusing to young children, and the child will more likely pay attention to the deed rather than the word. If adults want children to be giving, they must also be giving themselves.

The influence does not stop with being a good model, however. These techniques listed in the previous chapters are also

MODEL THE BEHAVIOR YOU EXPECT CHILDREN TO EXHIBIT

necessary in developing moral maturity. Nearly everyone knows of parents who are giving and kind but have children who are selfish and cruel. If the "model" were the only important influence, these children would more than likely be like their parents.

RESPECT YOURSELF AS WELL AS THE CHILD   Adults who allow children to be domineering and to do as they wish do not respect themselves. Consider the example of the little girl who acts up when company is in the home. She dances around the living room, asking her mother questions, asking her to get cookies and milk for her, interrupting her constantly. Mother ignores her and tries to carry on a conversation with the company, but her daughter is insistent and keeps up the attention-getting behavior.

If her mother continues to allow this behavior to continue, she is showing a lack of respect for herself as well as her company. On the other hand, she needs to maintain respect for her little girl. Spanking her or yelling at her would not be showing her respect. The mother should respond with something like "Mary, I have company right now, and you may stay in and visit with us if you can be quiet and let Mother talk. But if you choose to keep dancing and running around, you may take that behavior to the basement because we cannot visit when you are making so much noise. Which do you choose to do?"

The important step comes next in following through on the choice she has given the child. Often parents are able to verbalize the right words, but they do not stand by what they say, as we discussed earlier. If the child continues to run around and engage in attention-getting behavior, the mother should ask her whether she would like to go to the basement by herself or have her help her. Most children will respond at this point and behave as the parent expects. The child who has been subjected to disciplinary techniques showing disrespect for the child and the adult, however, will have a more difficult time at first responding in a situation where she is given a choice. As time goes on, however, she will become accustomed to this form of discipline and will begin to respond and will see herself and others as worthy of respect.

ALLOW CHILDREN TO MAKE CHOICES   The above illustration is a good example of how a child is allowed to make choices within a framework. Children should not be allowed to choose to do whatever they want. Limits of some sort need to be established. Children cannot, for example, choose whether they want to go to school, but they *can* choose what they will wear to school, what friends they will have at school, and what clubs they want to participate in. In the classroom children can be allowed to make decisions and choices about many parts of the curriculum and in doing so can begin to develop some of the behaviors most teachers set out to "teach" children—that is, development of a sense of responsibility, involvement in the curriculum, leadership ability, and development of critical thinking. Children will also acquire the ability to consider two sides to a problem and consequently will see another person's point of view. All these behaviors lead to moral maturity.

What specific kinds of choices can be made in the classroom and in the home? Many teachers feel uncomfortable giving choices to children because they like to be "in control" at all times, therefore making all decisions for children because they are "better qualified." Parents fall into the same "superiority" trap— believing the decisions *they* make must be better for the child because they are adults and certainly know what is "best." What adults do not realize is that children are capable of making decisions and that when they are allowed to become part of the decision-making process, the job of a parent or a teacher becomes much easier, since part of the responsibility is shared by the children.

Innumerable choices can be made by children in the classroom and in the home. Below are only a few:

At School

- choosing snacks
- choosing learning groups
- choosing disciplinary alternatives
- choosing stories
- choosing creative materials
- choosing creative projects
- choosing learning games
- choosing friends
- choices and decisions concerning classroom problems
- making decisions concerning the following:
  classroom policies
  field trips
  parties or special events
  special guests

At Home

- choosing clothing
- choosing play activities
- choosing menus for meals
- choosing special family outings
- making decisions concerning the following:
  family policies
  purchase of large items for the home
  work distribution
  discipline techniques
  family problems
  home decoration
  special occasions (holidays)
  vacations
  creative projects and materials

Suggested Choices or Decisions That Can Be Made by Young Children

purchase of classroom materials	friends
	meal times (a whole family decision)
	spending allowance

As we said earlier, it is extremely important that children be allowed to make decisions *within limits,* as will be discussed in the next section. Children need to be guided and trained to make responsible and wise decisions. However, adults should feel that they can allow a child to make a "wrong" decision, such as when the child's safety is not at stake. We all learn from making the "wrong" choice or decisions, and children should be allowed to experience making a wrong choice occasionally. Adults should carefully guide the child and help him see what the consequences of his decision might be. For example, a young boy cannot be allowed to decide whether he should stay outside and play in the rain in his new dress clothing and shoes. The adult can say, "Dave, you'll have to come in now because it is raining and you'll get your new clothes all wet and dirty. Would you like to run or walk to the house?" Another choice might be "Would you like to come to the back door or the basement door?" (Mother doesn't want the child to come in the front door because of the carpet).

CREATING FEELINGS OF ADEQUACY

Positive self-concepts require an atmosphere that creates a feeling of adequacy. Significant people influence this feeling. Feelings of adequacy create the motivation to perform and to accomplish important tasks of life. While it is necessary to provide information about what a child can successfully do, it is also possible to create a self-perception of inadequacy. A child's feeling of inadequacy results from comparisons with others who are more competent. Many times a child is told that he is incompetent or inadequate. A little reflection by the teacher will show that *every* human being adequately performs a large number of complex and difficult tasks that are found in the routine of human living. Being told that one is adequate can improve one's competency in a wide range of tasks.

The daughter of one of the authors found that she was having an extremely difficult time in a highly competitive elementary school attended mostly by the children of college professors. In this school she had not been able to compete successfully in a number of different academic areas. She had developed a belief that she was not competent in performing intellectual pursuits. As a result of these perceptions about herself, she was reluctant to undertake arithmetic, reading, and spelling assignments and, of course, did not want to complete her homework or participate in class. The next year, when the same girl attended school in a Polynesian culture, her parents were surprised one evening that she worked for two hours without interruption on some difficult math problems in her modern math sequence. She displayed enthusiasm, and when her father checked the work, he found she showed a great deal of insight. She completed the assignment the next day with 100 percent accuracy. After questioning their daughter and visiting with her teacher, her father found that she was one of the best students in reading and was doing very well in math. Only a few days of feeling adequate in a less-challenging school and having apparently been told by her teacher and friends that she was good in arithmetic had resulted in a remarkable change in her performance—both in the motivation and in the accuracy of the work.

Everyone needs to know what his limits are. It seems to be human nature to "push limits" as far as possible. Children need to know what their limits are in order to feel secure and loved. Teachers who do not set limits for children they teach are not preparing them for a world in which limits, rules, and laws are necessary for a happy and productive life. By setting limits, we are teaching a child to respect the rights and property of others. Limits should be set in such a way that a child still has freedom to act. For example, a teacher might say, "In a half hour it will be nap time. We *all* need to take naps. Would you like to work with the puzzles or with the blocks before we get ready to take naps?"

Teachers and parents must provide limits for the physical health and well-being of a child. For example, a teacher has great verbal, intellectual, and interpersonal skills, as well as full control over many important elements. However, growth is seen as a movement away from external controls and power. Limits should be developed by the child rather than being imposed from without.

As a child begins to mature, he becomes sensitive to the needs of others and identifies with them. Their welfare becomes important to him. It is this awareness that forms the basis of limits and self-control. The child finds that he cannot engage in certain behaviors without hurting others. He finds that certain statements or activities hurt his friends, siblings, and parents. Accordingly, he voluntarily imposes restraints upon himself so that his interpersonal relationships and the welfare of others are enhanced. It is not necessary for a parent

SET LIMITS

to reward or punish certain actions. Ethics and morality based on a more mature foundation of concern for others are not believed to result from simply applying the rod.

When a concern for others is developed, it becomes more rewarding than external reinforcers. Ethical behavior becomes a part of the child's concept of himself. A permanence of stability in his behavior results, transcending a system built on pleasure-seeking or fear of reprisals. But the reader may ask, "What about genuine conflicts between two persons, such as the parent and the child, when the child may suffer at the expense of the parent's demands, or vice-versa? Is it not so that at times the immediate interest of the parent and child are in direct opposition?" It is true that although the self-growth tendency of children and society's needs are generally compatible, in some instances they diverge and result in conflict. This is to be expected occasionally.

PROMOTE AUTONOMY

In order for parents and teachers to help children become morally autonomous, they must teach a child when he is very young to make choices and to act on his own.

First, they must *encourage the child's exposure to a wide range of information and experience.* An infant is dependent on adults because of his almost total lack of both physical and mental skills. He gradually develops these abilities. Because these skills are obtained through exposure to new information and experience, individuation requires that adults encourage such exposure. A child limited in his information about life is deprived of a number of avenues open to his growth. Thus, the process of becoming autonomous in any meaningful sense is retarded.

Second, *the adult also needs to be exposed to a wide range of information and experience.* As the child begins to individuate and to assert that individuality, he must be encouraged in this process by the continued respect and acceptance of the significant adults in his life. The child's individualization is facilitated if the adult is open to new information and change through new experience. If a teacher or parent is *not* open to new information and change, the child's attempts at being different or independent will be not only stifled but prohibited.

Finally, *adults should move, as much as is appropriately possible, from explicit rules to implicit rules.* That is, a child in the process of becoming different will respond better to "rules" that are simply assumed than to those that are carved in stone and "handed down."

Of course, everyone who works with young children realizes that because of the child's lack of experience and maturity, he

48

needs *some* explicit rules. Young children feel secure with limits. However, if the limits and rules become too severe, he feels very "closed in"; he can't make a move without breaking a rule. A list of too many explicit rules concerning care of books follows:

We do not tear the pages of the book.
We do not bend the cover back on the book.
We do not write on the book.
We do not throw the book on the floor.
We do not step on the book.
We do not take the book outside in the rain.
We do not put the book in the sink and get it wet.
We do not use the book with sticky fingers.
We do not cut the book with scissors.

As the reader can see, trying to establish explicit rules that cover everything about caring for books is overwhelming. A simple implicit rule such as "In this classroom, we have a rule that we *take good care of our books*" will suffice. Children should be allowed to think of specific ideas about *how* the implicit rule is to be applied. The teacher will then be encouraging independence and moral maturity.

In helping children respond to implicit rules as opposed to explicit rules, an adult should first establish *emotional bonding* by building a child's self-esteem and sense of being loved through acceptance and noncompetitive interaction with him. Children who do not respect and love an adult who presents implicit rules are less likely to respond positively.

The second step is to *model the behavior desired in the child*. For example, if there is an implicit rule in the home or school about taking care of books, and the adult leaves his or her books scattered around the house or in the car, the child will be confused and may model the opposite behavior. Also, a concern for questions of right and wrong can be modeled, communicated, and introduced into the environment, but not as explicit rules and sanctions. In this way the child becomes involved in defining and addressing moral problems and issues.

Teachers who are emotionally bonded to their children and who model and support the behavior they desire have much less need for explicit class rules, and thus they elicit less rebellion.

Analyze Experiences

In general, the role of the adult is to help the child intelligently analyze experiences not only in the home but when the child is with friends, in the classroom, and on the play-

49

ground. The responsibility for thinking is given to the child; the adult asks questions, models, clarifies, but does not provide moral clichés or conclusions. What the child must learn is how to identify a cause (selfishness) and to see the consequences of that act (being disliked). The skill is in the thinking, not in parroting the solution.

Adults should help children discern the consequences of their behavior on other children. For example, a parent or teacher points out that when a child shares with another, the other is happier. Or a parent or teacher may show that aggression toward another is producing fear, anger, and similar emotions. Moralizing becomes unnecessary, and negative reactions can be avoided.

Encourage Positive Actions

The classroom, or a home with several children, provides opportunities to have children participate in positive acts toward others. Such acts include sharing, working with others, completing work already started, and helping to attend to the injuries of others, either psychological or emotional. Direct assignment of responsibility to a child is an especially potent method for developing both behavioral and cognitive maturity. By learning the roles of others, a child will acquire a sensitivity to their feelings that will help him understand their needs and goals. The child can explore the behaviors of various roles in our culture, such as a parent, a policeman, a fireman, and others. Using role playing in the classroom, a teacher can teach a problem-solving approach to social difficulties and moral problems.

Whether you are a teacher or a parent, remember these steps in enacting role playing in the classroom or at home. First, present the problem. Next, select children to be role players. Then prepare the audience to participate as observers by telling them what to look for and what to discuss after the role-playing episode. Set the stage, provide props, and give brief guiding instructions just before the enactment. Now allow the children to act out the role. Follow up with discussion and evaluation.

In the above procedural steps, the most critical skill will be that of allowing the role players to make their own decisions. During the discussion, the children's views should be respected even when they depart from what the adult might wish. After trial and error, children will be willing to leave behind immature reactions. Through patient guidance, they will come to decide for themselves that they are inappropriate.

50

The teacher or parent should provide an atmosphere conducive to effective role playing—one in which little criticism or evaluation exists. This freedom from evaluation allows children to feel safe in exploring both antisocial and social behavior. During role playing children should feel free to express strong feelings, even negative ones, as a mode of learning. The teacher's role is to encourage, not direct, the discussion following role playing.

SUMMARY

In summary, a number of classroom and home activities and procedures will provide a climate conducive to moral development. Such a climate is characterized by freedom, acceptance, and trust—necessary ingredients for the development of a problem-solving approach to human interaction.

PART 2
PRACTICAL
APPLICA-
TIONS

Chapters in this section describe practical applications of the principles discussed in section one. Each chapter consists of a brief review of a principle, followed by a presentation of stories and techniques for teaching the principle. The discerning adult is expected to select those techniques that best fit his or her teaching situation. A combination of techniques is considered to be most effective.

A discussion of alternatives and possible solutions to real problems or hypothetical situations is effective in helping children make moral decisions. Moreover, an adult can gain insight into the level of a child's moral thinking and can observe any changes or progress in that thinking.

For example, if a child responds to a "conflict" story by telling the adult that a spanking is the solution, that child is functioning on the lowest level of moral development—the level of punishment and obedience.

If, on the other hand, the child, after role playing to develop empathy, responds that the two involved should cooperate in order to be treated nicely, he or she has progressed to the second stage of moral development—self-reward, or hedonism. The third stage of development is also involved here: seeking the approval of others.

The child is progressing when he responds that the children involved should conform to an authority figure, that "this is the rule at our school, and the teacher says we should."

But the ultimate goal for any teacher or parent is to obtain an altruistic response from a child—a response that clearly reveals the child is concerned with individual rights, such as working out some kind of agreement equitable to both role players. At this level the child wants to do what is "right," based on the feelings, needs, and desires of all concerned and on the way the decision affects the environment and society surrounding them.

Obviously, the goal is to help a child progress from lower to higher stages of moral maturity and responsibility.

5
HELPING A CHILD UNDER-STAND OTHERS

How do children learn to understand others? Why do some people *never* learn to understand others? We have all had the feeling of not being understood by someone. The typical responses, "He just doesn't understand me," and "She has no feelings for others," exemplify the way many of us have felt in these situations. Typically, little children lack an understanding of others. They are egocentric and have not had enough experience in the world to relate to the needs and problems of other people. It is our firm belief, however, that young children can be helped to understand the feelings of others. The following principles will be discussed as they relate to understanding others.

- Empathy
- Altruism
- Intentionality
- Flexibility

These principles will be illustrated with stories that can be used in helping young children internalize them.

Empathy is developed when a person is able to "feel" for other persons and to put himself "in their shoes." This is a difficult achievement for young children because their natural egocentricity causes them to think of themselves first. How does empathy develop in a young child?

It can develop very early. Infants are first able to sense their parents' positive and negative feelings, and this ability later

EMPATHY AND ALTRUISM

55

generalizes to other people. Small infants are happy when their mothers are holding them. These early reactive emotions in the infant cannot be called empathic, however. They are simply emotional reactions. The child is not assumed to know anything about the physical or emotional state of the parent.

Next the infant learns that certain behaviors are almost invariably associated with the relief of his own distress and that of his parents. For example, cuddling often serves to relieve an infant's distress. Smiles and winks are also associated with the relief of distress. Later, sharing toys, giving food and drink, and rocking are acts that the young child will begin to associate with positive emotional reactions or reduction of unpleasant reactions in those around him. Thus, the child is learning what actions make him happy. The child may also be learning what events make the parents happy.

But the infant and the very young child do not really know where the self stops and the "not-me" begins. Is the end of my finger the end of me, or do I continue into the blocks I play with and the mother with whom I cuddle? Am I always one, or do I separate into parts with space between? We see mother and child, but the young child likely sees only himself, sometimes as a composite of himself and his mother—and possibly including part of the inanimate world that surrounds him.

The child has gone through two stages of growth. First, he has learned some initial distress feelings, probably picked up from his mother. Second, he has learned to associate certain behaviors with changes in his own emotions. The child's growth phase is also characterized by a growing awareness that his existence is separate from others. This separate existence need only be an emotional awareness, that is, the child will now learn that his own emotions do not exactly match the emotional state of others. True empathy arises during the third stage. The child shares emotional states with others, becoming aware of antecedent causes and typical modes of relief.

Empathy is defined as the sharing of emotional states. Empathy is an emotional reaction caused by awareness of another emotion. The very young child does not perceive others as separate from himself. Based on our definition, his emotional reaction is probably not empathy. Empathy requires more than the mere observation of *behavior*, it requires the perception of *emotion*. This usually requires interpretation by the observer, and may be confused because the projection of the observer's own emotional state onto the other. True empathy means he is reacting emotionally to his *perception* of the emotion of others.

Along with emotional capabilities, the child learns that his emotions are different from those of others. But he learns that relief to others brings him relief. Up to this point in his young life the child has acted primarily to relieve only his own feelings.

The primary basis for the genuine helping act is empathy. Empathy is the emotional state that can automatically result when one perceives the emotional state of another. This perception might be based either directly on the facial and verbal expressions of the distressed person or indirectly on other kinds of cues, such as the words of other bystanders. Empathy is restricted to the emotional state aroused *solely* by the perception of the other's experience. Imagine a frightening situation in which two people are equally scared, but one manages to help the other escape. By most standards such an act would be termed altruistic. But it is not, if the helping person's emotions were aroused by the situational forces and not by the perception of the other's emotions.

Putting these criteria for empathy and altruism together, we get a rather strict interpretation of what constitutes an instance of altruism. Empathy can arise only through the perception of another's experience independent of one's own situation, and the ensuing altruistic act can be called altruistic only if it is motivated by the desire to relieve the other's distress, and not by the desire for possible social approval, reciprocity, equity, expected rewards, fear of castigation, and guilt, among other reasons.

The child acquires the sympathetic and altruistic disposition gradually as the result of socialization. He is not born with these dispositions. Their acquisition is open to all the errors and trials that confront other tasks of maturation and learning. For convenience, we divide this developmental process into three steps; but keep in mind that the process is continuous, with some aspects of the child's behavior falling at once into all three stages.

First: The child must learn to associate changes in his emotional state with concrete external events including social cues and expressions of others. Thus, if Mommy is suddenly made cheerful due to affectionate behavior from father, *and* the child simultaneously experiences a change in emotion, and if such events occur often, the child will come to associate the two events together. It is possible that after such visual associations have been formed, each time the child sees them they will elicit the same or a similar emotional change as before. This, of course, is classical conditioning.

Second, these social cues that elicit positive emotions must become associated with acts of helping. The child learns that some of his actions will be followed by changes in these external, observable, social cues. (Later, he may come to know of these social cues through words, but he first must observe them.)

Once these two events have been established—(a) a child's emotions attached to social cues, and (b) knowledge that helping actions will be followed by social cues—altruistic acts may be expected. The altruistic acts will produce expressive social cues, and the social cues will now produce positive emotions in the altruist to relieve unpleasant emotions or create positive feelings.

Some basic elements can play a role in the establishment of a connection that elicits a desired emotional state in the helping child.

Following the first two conditions—(a) identification of emotional states; and (b) positive emotions becoming associated with helping—a third element enters. With an increased ability to conceptualize his word, to think, remember, recall, meditate, understand, create, imagine, and otherwise engage in behaviors of the mind, *the intrinsic value of sympathetic acts* may gain mental representation. Since the child has undoubtedly recognized the consequences of the acts on others, he can mentally anticipate the beneficial outcome *for* others of such acts. It is quite likely that the value idea will be coupled to the outcome idea, thus forming a kind of altruistic motivation. Practice in responding altruistically and witnessing distress cues in others finally gives the helping behavior a kind of independent status. That is to say, altruistic behavior at last comes to be emitted without much thought of personal reward or gain; it becomes authentic altruism.

While these formulations are not simple, we believe they contribute to a general understanding of the developmental processes involved in the acquisition of altruistic behavior. Based on the preceding theory, the following instructional techniques are proposed:

1. Calling to attention the *needs* of another individual.
   "Homer was very *hungry* and you ate all the sausages before he could get one."
2. Calling to attention the *feelings* of another individual.
   "Homer felt very *sad* when you ate all the sausages. He was hungry and now he doesn't have anything to eat."
3. Help the child try to *put himself in the shoes of the other individual.*

58

"Try to think what it would be like if you were very hungry and you wanted a sausage very much and someone ate them all. Would you be happy or sad? Would you still be hungry?"

4. Help the child *discover* his feelings but avoid lecturing or telling the child how he would feel if the same thing happened to him. Ask the child questions which are neither probing, sarcastic, or humiliating. The tone of the voice is important in helping the child discover feelings on his own.

   Say, "I wonder how it would feel to be hungry and plan on eating sausages and then find out that someone already ate them all? I wonder if you would feel happy or sad? I wonder if you would still be hungry? Would you feel angry?"

   Do Not Say, "I'm sure if someone ate all your sausages that you would feel sad or angry. It's not nice to eat other people's food when they are planning on eating it. You would be very angry if someone did that to you."

   The above example tells the child how *you think* he should feel and does not allow the child the opportunity to discover these feelings *on his own*.

   It is important that children become increasingly knowledgeable about the thoughts, feelings, and motives of other people. "Roletaking is a necessary condition for the development of conventional moral thought." This statement suggests, logically enough, that since most moral evaluations involve others as either actor or acted upon, the ability to view an event as another would is deemed a necessary condition to judging that event. Piaget noted that young children have difficulties placing themselves in another's position or seeing an event through the eyes of another person; the child is unconsciously centered upon himself or herself (1967, p. 21). He or she is unable to take another's point of view, Piaget says, and not until a child is seven to twelve years old is he or she able to coordinate his or her view with the viewpoints of others. We believe that this skill can occur at even younger ages but Piaget's basic observations are correct.

5. Help the child to *act* upon the feelings of empathy. In other words, helping a child learn that a feeling of empathy is important but is not enough, a person must *respond* to that feeling. *Altruism* is the term used to describe a person's behaviors that relieve the distress of another individual. This behavior is motivated by the child's feeling of empathy and honest desire to help relieve another's distress, not by a de-

sire for social approval, expected rewards, or fear of punishment. The expression of altruism is a mature moral response and not typically developed at a young age. Movement toward altruism can be made, however, by the child's first developing the feeling of empathy and, second, by encouraging the child to *act* upon that feeling. If a child sees another child fall of a tricycle and the child feels empathy for the hurt child, he should also then be encouraged to respond by lifting the hurt child and attending to any injuries. Often a young child can and does show altruistic responses. Adults need to be attentive to these responses by rewarding the child and helping him to feel good for responding to the needs of another in distress. The development of empathy and feeling for another individual is incomplete without acting upon that feeling. Children need to be encouraged to respond to the needs of others solely for the reason of helping another individual. In the illustration used above with Homer and the sausages, a response on the part of the adult might be:

"I wonder if we could think of a way to help Homer so he won't feel sad or hungry any more. Can we find him some more sausages or can you think of something else we could do?"

Many young children are able to feel empathy and to express altruistic responses even though both are considered to be mature responses. Why is this so? Altruism and empathy can function on an emotional level as well as on a mental, logical level. In considering the developmental level of the child, we could say that the young child is not really at a thinking level in which he can express altruism, yet emotionally he can. Consider the following real life example:

Falling Out of the Car   The family was riding home from church with a friend. When the car turned the corner, Dallas, who was sitting in the back seat with two of his brothers, leaned against the door handle, making the door fly open. Dallas tumbled out of the car and hit the pavement. Immediately Randy, the older brother (about 8 years old), jumped out of the car to help Dallas. Before Mother could respond, Randy had helped Dallas to the side of the road and out of the way of the oncoming traffic. His response was much faster and more helpful than that of Mother, who seemed to be frozen in the front seat.

60

Another true example of altruism in a young child involves a hurt finger. Most young children have been hurt before, so they can relate the action to internal feelings. Express empathy for someone else who has been hurt.

Allen found a "trick" nail in a box of cereal and decided to trick his little cousin, Jeremy, age two. Allen put the nail on his finger in such a way that the nail appeared to be going through his finger. When he showed Jeremy his finger, acting of course as if it were hurting very much, Jeremy responded with "Oh, does it hurt? I will go with you to tell your mommy." Jeremy expressed not only empathy but altruism when he desired to relieve the imagined distress of Allen and help him find his mommy. This type of behavior is emotionally mature for a young child.

What then happens to young children who at an early age are able to express feelings of empathy and altruism and later become selfish and self-centered and appear unable to express empathic and altruistic feelings? It appears that selfishness is learned from the environment. Even though a young child's tendency is to be self-centered or egocentric, these traits may not necessarily lead to selfishness. However, as parents and teachers model selfishness and defensiveness and inadvertently reward these attributes, children will gradually become less empathic and altruistic. It appears then that the two enemies to empathy and altruism are (1) defensiveness—or protection of the self; focusing on protection of self-esteem to an excess; and (2) the rewarding of selfishness and encouragement to think of the self first.

What is the cure for the above "selfishness disease?" Like any disease, the older one gets and the longer the person has the disease, the harder it is to cure; so ideally, the best time is when a child is young. Reinforcing those empathic and altruistic responses when they do occur, helping the child feel good about what he has done, is one prevention. Also, trying to "create" situations in which the child can respond empathetically. Avoid an atmosphere of competitiveness and self-interest. Role playing, as we mentioned before, is an extremely useful tool. Telling stories and creating conflict situations or moral dilemmas in which the child is asked to respond can encourage him to develop empathy.

The following stories can be used with young children to help them develop empathy.

I. *Discussion Questions:*

1. Why did John feel sad when his crayons dropped?
2. Would you feel sad if you dropped your crayons?
3. What would you do if you dropped your new crayons all over the road?
4. What would you do if you were John's friend?
5. Did Shane do a good thing when he brought John some of his crayons from home?
6. If you were Shane, would you bring new crayons to your friend?

II. *Role Playing:*

Let the children select the parts they would like to play. The adult will read the story as they act it out. The second time, have the children verbalize the parts as they remember them. Children learn through repetition; therefore, the role-playing may need to be repeated several times to allow all the interested children to participate.

III. Make up stories or tell true stories that have happened to the children.

John was happy today. He had a new box of crayons to bring to school. John loved to color, but he didn't have very many colors in his old box. Now he had a brand new box, and he was so proud. John was looking at his crayons on the bus while he was riding to school. He was showing all the pretty colors to Shane, his best friend. "See how many colors I have in my new box of crayons, Shane," said John. "You better be careful," said Shane, "or you might drop them!"

John carefully put the crayons back in the box because it was almost time to get off the bus. The bus stopped in front of the school; Shane and John got in line. Just as John was about to step down the steps of the bus, the boy in back of him ran into him because the girl in back of him ran into him, and so on. One of the big boys in the back of the bus had pushed a child, and everybody had run into everybody else. John fell, and all his crayons fell down the steps of the bus. "Keep moving," the bus driver said.

"But my crayons," said John. "They fell all over the street. I have to pick them up. They are all new." John started to cry.

"Keep moving," said the bus driver. "I still have another load of kids to pick up."

As the children filed out of the bus, they stepped all over John's crayons until they were all broken.

"My crayons are all ruined," cried John. "I'll never have any new crayons, ever."

Shane felt very sad for his best friend, John. That night when Shane was getting ready for bed, he asked mother to get him a paper bag. "What for?" asked mother.

"I need to take some crayons to school," said Shane.

"Why?" asked mother. "Don't you already have some crayons at school?"

"Yes," said Shane, "but these are for my friend, John. His crayons are all old and broken and stepped on."

"Oh," said mother. "Well, I guess that would be okay. You have a lot of crayons anyway."

The next day Shane brought a bag of new crayons for John, and John was very happy. "Thanks, Shane," said John. "You are my very best friend."

I. *Discussion Questions:*

1. Why did the boys let the frogs go?
2. Do you think it was a good thing to do?
3. How do you think you would feel if you were put into a jar?
4. Would you feel happy or sad?
5. Would you like to get out of the jar?
6. How do you think the frogs felt?

II. *Role playing:*

Let the children select the parts they would like to play and have the teacher or the parent read the story. The story can be acted out several times in order to give the children a chance to participate if they would like to.

Note: It is important for the adult using the above story to remember that the purpose of this story is *not to scare* children into doing the empathic thing. The *object* is to help the children understand the feelings of another—in this case of the frogs—which will help the child to gain a feeling of empathy for the distressed and respond in an altruistic manner. Letting the frogs go

Randy and Allen were out playing on the porch that mother had just washed down with the hose. They were having a wonderful time slipping and sliding on the wet cement. All of a sudden, four frogs hopped out of a hole in the wooden frame around the porch. The boys were so excited. For awhile they slid around the porch chasing the frogs. The frogs jumped very high and as they landed, they splashed water all over the boys. What great fun Randy and Allen were having with the frogs.

Then Randy had a great idea. "I know, Allen. Let's catch the frogs and put them in a bottle. Then tomorrow we can take them out and play with them again."

"That will be fun," said three-year-old Allen. So Randy ran to the kitchen and brought out a big jar of mother's. The boys chased and chased the frogs until they finally caught three of them. One frog jumped away and went back down into the hole he had come from.

The boys were happy watching the frogs in the bottle for most of the afternoon. When mother came out and saw the frogs she said, "Boys, don't you think it would be better to let the frogs go?"

"No." responded Randy and Allen. "We had to work hard to catch these frogs and we want to play with them tomorrow." So mother proceeded to tell Randy and Allen a make-believe story.

*   *   *   *   *

(or suggesting to let the frogs go) because of fear is not the object in using the above story.

III. *New Stories:*

Let the children make up their own stories dealing with empathy, or discuss something that has actually happened to them.

"Let me tell you a story about two little boys the same age as you, who found themselves in a strange land. The boys, named Jim and Stan, were out walking one day, and after awhile they became lost. They walked and walked until they came to a big field of grass. Suddenly they saw three giant frogs coming toward them and discovered that they were in a giant-frog land. Jim and Stan ran and ran and ran, but they couldn't get away from the giant frogs. Suddenly one of the frogs caught Jim. Another frog caught Stan. In frog language they said, "Hey, look at these little boys we found. Let's put them in a jar and keep them until tomorrow and then we can play with them.""

Jim and Stan were very sad. They were afraid of the frogs and they were worried that their mothers would not know where they were, so they squirmed and kicked, but they still could not get away.

The frogs put the boys in a glass jar and fed them bugs and grass but the boys did not like bugs and grass and were very hungry. How they wished they were home with their mother and father. How they wished they could eat some spaghetti or hamburgers and french fries. What would they ever do? If the frogs did not let them go, they would surely die. The boys started to cry. They felt sad for their parents, too, because they knew how sad their parents would be when their little boys did not return home.

As the boys were wiping away their tears and trying to think of a plan to escape, the frogs' mother came out to see what her little boy frogs were doing. When she saw that the frogs had captured two little boys and put them in a bottle, she said, "Now you frogs, let those little boys go. How would you feel if some big boys caught you and put you in a jar and wouldn't let you go?"

"We wouldn't like it." said the frogs. "Then we couldn't hop around and catch bugs. I guess we will let the boys go, but we sure did want to play with them tomorrow."

The boys were so happy. When the frogs let them go they ran and ran until they found some nice people. They told the people their names, and the people called their mother. Mother came to get them.

Jim and Stan were finally home again and could eat people food. "We will never walk far away from home again," they said.

*   *   *   *   *

After telling Randy and Allen the story of the giant frogs, mother walked into the kitchen. Randy and Allen thought and thought. Then with a quick glance at Allen, Randy opened the lid to the jar containing the frogs and let them hop out. The frogs seemed glad to get out of the jar and hopped very high. They reached the hole in the wood frame on the porch and returned to where they had come from when mother washed the porch.

6
UNDER-STANDING THE INTENTIONS OF OTHERS

When an adult asks a young child, "Did you do that on purpose?" the child may not know what "on purpose" really means. As adults, we can evaluate acts in terms of the motives or intentions of the acting person, but a very young child cannot. He is unable to distinguish his own perspective from the viewpoint of another (this is egocentrism). Therefore, when evaluating the seriousness of a moral act, a child will focus on the amount of damage done rather than upon the intentions motivating the act. For example, if you tell a child a story in which one child broke two cups while climbing in the cupboard to steal some cookies, and another child broke ten cups accidentally when he tripped and fell over the dog, the child evaluates the seriousness of the acts according to the amount of damage done. The "worst" child, then, was the child who broke ten cups. The fact that it was an accident does not seem to make any difference to the child because of his lack of ability to focus on two dimensions of the same act.

According to Piaget, as a child reaches a higher level of moral development, he or she will learn to consider why a person acted as he did. Less importance will be placed on the consequences or the amount of damage.

Helping children understand the intentions of others can aid in developing in them a basic understanding of others. Children need to understand intentionality in order to develop acceptance and empathy. Caution should be used, however, in teaching this concept to young children so that they are not taught that because a person did not do something intentionally, that makes it right. In other words, *accidentally* knocking another child to the floor does not make knocking children to the floor right. We can *understand,* however, that the child did not do it on purpose, and therefore he should not be judged harshly.

In teaching children to understand the intentions of others, teachers and parents can do the following:

1. *Read stories*: containing moral dilemmas about intentionality.

2. *Ask questions*: such as "Which of the children is naughtier?" and "Why?" ask other discussion questions, as listed following previous stories. Adults should be careful not to provide the answers to the questions but should help children discover the answers themselves. Adults should also try to help children show a gradual preference for considering intentions when they evaluate an act.

   Children should not be forced to answer; if they do not reply, simply move on to another story. Unwillingness to answer does not mean the child has not been stimulated or influenced by the story and the questions. Often, after a child has given the story and the questions some deep thought, he will surprise the adult with an expression of enlightened opinion. Questions such as the following might be used: "Which child wanted to hurt her brother? Which child wanted to help? Who had an accident? Who was doing something bad on purpose? Who was trying to do the right thing?"

3. *Role play*: one of the stories and allow the children to play a number of different roles.

One day the children at the nursery school were playing with the Legos. Jerry wanted *all* the Legos for himself and started grabbing all the other children's Legos. While he was fighting with Keith, trying to take his Legos away, he pinched Keith's finger, and Keith cried. Pretty soon Keith was better, though.

Richard wanted to play with the Legos too, and he asked Doris if she would share her Legos with him. "Okay," said Doris. As Richard walked over to get some Legos from Doris, he accidently stepped on Jeff's hand and smashed his fingers. Jeff cried and cried, and the teacher had to call his mother to come and get him because he was hurt so bad.

Discussion Questions:

1. Which child was naughtier? Jerry, who wanted all the Legos and hurt Keith's finger a little while taking his Legos, or Richard, who asked Doris to share her Legos and hurt Jeff's fingers very badly while walking over to get the Legos from Doris?
2. Which child *asked* for the Legos?
3. Which child *took* the Legos?
4. Is it better to take Legos or ask for them?
5. Who was hurt the most?
6. Did Jerry *mean* to hurt Jeff?
7. Which child *meant* to be mean to the other children?
8. Who had an accident?
9. Who did something bad on purpose?
10. How would you feel if someone took all your Legos and hurt your finger?
11. How would you feel if you stepped on someone's finger accidentally and they were really hurt?

Discussion Questions:

1. Which child was naughtier? Laura who threw some soapy water in Lester's eyes or Jane who spilled the beans all over the floor?
2. Which child was doing something helpful?
3. Which child tried to hurt another child?
4. Which child meant to do something naughty?
5. Who had an accident?
6. Which child did something bad on purpose?
7. How would you feel if you had spilled the beans?
8. How would you feel if your sister threw soapy water in your eyes?

One day mother went to lunch with some friends. She left a nice lunch for Laura and the other children and asked them to clean things up when they were finished eating. After lunch the children said, "Let's clean things up nice and clean so Mother will be happy." So the children started to clean up the kitchen and put the dishes in the sink.

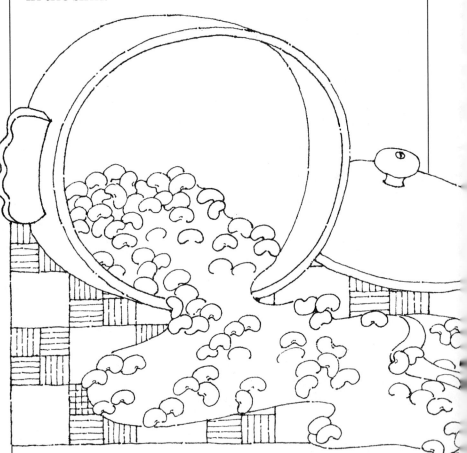

Laura decided to be the one to wash the dishes. She got the sink full of nice, soapy water. As she was washing the dishes, Lester, her younger brother came over, carrying some dirty silverware. "Here," he said, giving the silverware to Laura. Laura could not resist the temptation to throw some soapy water in Lester's eyes. Lester started to cry, but soon his eyes were all better.

Jane was carrying a big pan of beans over to the cabinet. She was trying to be careful and not spill a drop. Just as she got near the cabinet, she tripped over her sister's doll that was lying on the floor, and she spilled the beans all over the floor. "You dummy," said Laura. "Now see what you have done. You have spilled the beans all over the floor, and we have no more. Mother was going to have those beans for supper tonight. Look at the mess you made, too. It will take us an hour to clean this up. Boy, will Mother be mad."

Discussion Questions:

1. Which child was naughtier? John who *poured* the half glass of juice on Sherry's lap, or Richard who accidentally knocked over Paul's glass of juice and Kathy's glass of juice too?
2. Who had an accident?
3. Who did something wrong on purpose?
4. Which child was doing something helpful?
5. Which child *meant* to do something helpful?
6. Is it all right to pour juice on people's laps?
7. Is it all right to spill juice accidentally?
8. How would you feel if you had spilled two people's juice accidentally?
9. How would you feel if someone poured juice on your lap?
10. Do we all have accidents sometimes?

It was snack time in the nursery school, and the children were sitting around the table having orange juice and crackers.

John decided it would be funny to pour juice on Sherry's lap. So he poured about half a glass on her lap. Sherry cried and called the teacher. The teacher came over and wiped up the orange juice from Sherry's lap.

Richard asked the teacher to pass the juice. As he reached to pick up the pitcher of juice to pour some into his glass, he knocked over a whole glass of juice that belonged to Paul, sitting next to him. Paul cried because the juice got all over him. Richard reached to get a napkin to help wipe up the juice on Paul, and he accidentally knocked over Kathy's juice. Now there were two glasses of juice spilled and two children wet with orange juice.

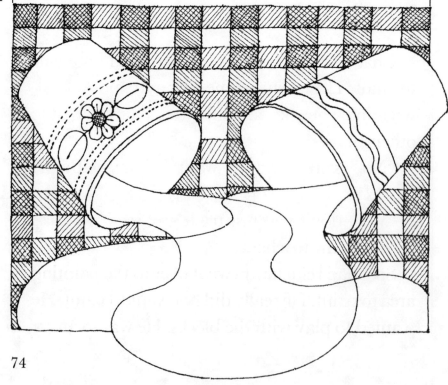

The children at the nursery school were painting pictures. Some were using crayons and some were using paints. They were using all kinds of pretty colors—red, blue, purple, yellow, and green.

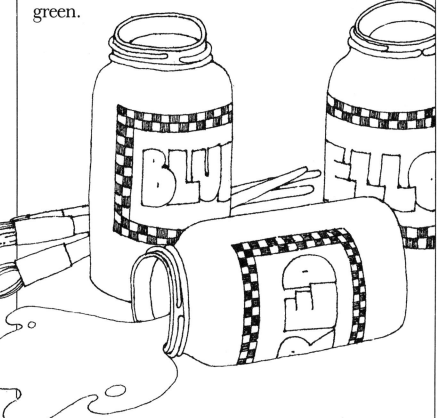

Chad was in the block area and did not want to paint. The teacher came over and said, "Chad, wouldn't you like to come and paint with the other children?"

"No," said Chad. "I want to play with the blocks."

"Why don't you just try it and see if you like it?" asked the teacher.

So Chad reluctantly went over to the painting area to paint. He really did not want to paint. He wanted to play with the blocks. He was so angry

STORY #4
PAINTING
PICTURES

Discussion Questions:

1. Which child was naughtier? Chad who poured the paint on the table, or Daniel who spilled two jars of paint while cleaning up the other spilled paint?
2. Which child was trying to help?
3. Which child did something naughty on purpose?
4. Is it worse to spill two colors of paint while cleaning up, or to spill one color of paint on purpose?
5. Who had an accident?
6. Was it okay for Chad to spill the paint on the table because he didn't want to paint but wanted to play in the blocks?
7. How would you feel if you were trying to help and you knocked over the blue and the yellow paint and spilled them?

about having to paint that when the teacher gave him some bright red paint, he poured it all over the table.

When Daniel saw that Chad had poured the paint on the table, he ran to get a sponge to help clean up the mess. When he came back to the table and started to clean up the spilled paint, he accidentally knocked over a big jar of yellow paint and a big jar of blue paint. Oh, what a mess now!

Angela was coloring with a package of sixteen crayons. Her picture did not turn out like she wanted, so she threw the package of crayons on the floor. The crayons spilled all over.

Kathy was helping the teacher by passing out the crayons to the other children. She had a big pail with about 100 crayons in it. As she was passing them out, she tripped over the leg of a chair and fell and spilled all the crayons on the floor.

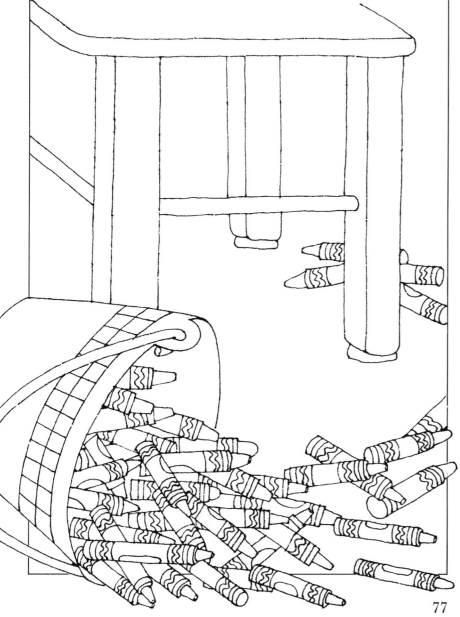

STORY #5
SPILLING
CRAYONS

Discussion Questions:

1. Which girl was naughtier, Angela who threw a package of sixteen crayons on the floor, or Kathy, who tripped and fell and spilled a bucket of 100 crayons?
2. Which child spilled the most crayons?
3. Is it worse to spill more crayons or is it worse to throw crayons on the floor on purpose?
4. Did the child who tripped and spilled the big bucket of crayons *mean* to, or did she spill them accidentally?
5. Is it bad to spill crayons accidentally?
6. Who was trying to help?
7. Who did something naughty on purpose?
8. Who had an accident?
9. How would you feel if you were helping the teacher and tripped and spilled all the crayons? Would you feel happy or sad?

77

7
FLEXIBILITY

Typically, a young child's thinking is rigid and inflexible. He sees things as black or white, right or wrong, good or bad. He has a difficult time seeing the "grays" or understanding that some things are not completely good or completely bad, completely wrong or completely right.

One area in which children have a difficult time being flexible is in the area of breaking promises. Though parents and teachers should be consistent, trying their best to follow through with promises made to children and not making promises they do not think they can keep, the time comes in every adult's life when he cannot keep a promise. This is a difficult situation for a child to handle, and the adult often hears "But you promised!" when it is understandable both to the child and the adult that the promise cannot be kept. Consider the following real-life examples:

Going to the Movie: The family had planned to go to the drive-in for a special family night activity. Everyone was ready to go and were waiting in the car. When dad came out to start the car, nothing happened. The car wouldn't start. Dad worked and worked to get the car started, but it wouldn't start. Dad said, "Sorry, kids. I guess we can't go tonight. Maybe next week." "But you promised!" cried the children.

Field Trip to the Duck Pond: The children were all getting very excited about their school field trip to the duck pond. They were going to take their lunch and spend the whole day at the pond feeding the ducks and throwing in stones. The day finally came. But it rained, and the field trip was called off. "Sorry, children," said the teacher. "Maybe we can go in several days when the weather clears up." "But you promised," said the children.

Baking Cookies: "Mommy, could we bake some colored sugar cookies today? Red is my favorite color," said Shane. "Yes, I think we can, Shane. I have a few things to do now, but probably later we can bake the cookies," said Mother. Mother did her work and was thinking about getting the things ready to bake the cookies as she and Shane had planned. The phone rang and Mother answered. It was an old friend who was coming to town and would be coming to spend the evening. Mother had to hurry and fix a nice supper and prepare the house for guests. "What about the cookies, Mom?" asked Shane. "Shane, I'm afraid we won't be able to make them now because we are going to have company for supper. Mommy doesn't have time now." "But Mom, you promised," whined Shane. Shane simply could *not* understand why, when his mother had promised to bake cookies, she wouldn't follow through with the plan. He could only see his own needs and not those of the others involved.

*   *   *   *   *

Training for Flexibility

How, then, do we train children to think less rigidly and to be more flexible? The following suggestions can be of value in helping a child become morally mature:

1. *Try to be consistent most of the time* and follow through with promises you make to the children. But be careful about what is promised so you can *plan* to follow through with the promise most of the time. Many adults make promises as a bribe, with no intention of following through. This is a difficult situation for children to handle because they feel they cannot trust the adult or count on what he says. Unfortunately, many adults use moods to change the arranged plans. "I just don't feel like taking you kids to the show today. I know I promised, but I am the mother and I have the right to change my mind if I want to. Maybe some other time." How often have children heard that one? Occasionally that statement is valid, but if a mother uses it often, her child learns not to believe what she says.

2. *Behavior should be based on rationality.* Adults need to be careful not to change the rules for their own personal needs or desires but only for rational, logical reasons. These reasons should be explained to children. "Shane, I know you had counted on making the cookies today and so did I, but some friends just called and will be coming for dinner. There simply isn't time now."

80

3. Show children that *being flexible can also work in a positive way*. For example, adults often issue ultimatums they are not always able to follow through with, such as the following:
   - *Eating cereal*: "In this house there will be no sugar cereal. It is bad for the teeth, it is expensive, and it is not nutritious." Many adults have such a rule, but are found "giving in" on special occasions, or when the cereal is on sale, or when mother goes to the hospital. Do the children complain that their parents are not following through with the promise of not having cereal in the house? No, they accept the decision with no complaint.
   - *Drinking soft drinks*: "In this house we will not drink soft drinks because they are bad for the teeth; they are expensive; they contain high amounts of sugar, which is not good for the body; and some contain caffeine." Again, such a rule exists in many homes, yet parents give in by buying drinks when the drinks are on sale, when the family goes on trips, when they have birthday parties, and when company comes to dinner. Again, the children will probably not complain about such an inconsistent rule.
   - *Going to the movie*: "No, you can't go to the movie tonight because you were out late last night, and we can't afford it," said mother. "But Mother, my friend invited me and tonight is the last night it will be on." "No," said Mother. "'I said no!" Later on, Mother changed her mind when she thought that the movie was only on one more night and her child's friend had invited him. Did the child complain that Mother had changed her mind in this case? No, of course not.

   Children should be reminded that sometimes their parents' flexibility works in a positive way that will benefit them.
4. *Modeling or example*: Adults should model being flexible and being able to accept disappointments and changes in plans without getting upset. Adults who get terribly upset when their plans do not work out are not setting a good example for their children. It is likely the children will follow their example.
5. *Use humor on appropriate occasions*: One day our family had planned to go water skiing in our new boat, purchased at the beginning of the summer. We decided to take a good friend along who was eager to learn to water ski. The boat had been in the boat repair shop the week before, but the repairman had assured us it would be fixed in time for us to water ski on Saturday. When we all arrived at the boat dock, ready for a full day of water skiing, the boat did not

seem to be anywhere in sight. Where was it? A quick trip to the boat repair shop answered the question. It was still not repaired. That meant we could not go water skiing that day. Everyone was upset except for the good friend we had brought along. She was a good sport and said, "Well, we can have fun swimming, anyway." The children could not seem to stop complaining about the incident and kept expressing their disappointment about the boat. We told them about the fun we could have swimming and how we could water ski next week. All the children finally seemed satisfied except one child, who continued to complain.

We drove the van around to the other side of the lake where the swimming was, and our friend saw that Randy still was not going to be satisfied with the situation. As my friend Linda got out of the van, she decided to use a little humor to relieve the tension. She started hitting the van with two fists and said laughingly, "I'm so disappointed you couldn't get the boat to use today. You big dummy! I'm never going to come out with you again. I've been planning all week to go water skiing, and now you have messed up everything." When Randy saw how funny her remarks were and how ridiculous it was to complain about something that could not be helped, he stopped complaining and accepted the fact that we could not go water skiing that day and would have a good time swimming.

Stories to Illustrate Flexibility:
(Refer to the stories listed under the following titles.)
- Going to the movie
- Field trip to the duck pond
- Baking cookies
- Eating cereal
- Drinking soft drinks
- Going to the movie
- Using humor
- Cleaning up

I. *Discussion Questions* (ask these questions after *each* story):
1. What was supposed to happen?
2. Did it happen?
3. Did things go the way they were supposed to?
4. Did the people in the story get angry or happy? Why?
5. Was it a good idea to change their minds?
6. How would you feel if something like this happened to you?
7. How did the grownup feel?

II. *Role Play*:

Allow each child to participate and to play different roles.

III. *Make up additional stories.*

*STORY #1
CLEANING
UP*

Questions:

1. How do you think Keith responded?
2. What do you think was right?
3. Who was right and who was wrong?
4. What should the teacher have done?
5. Why do you think the boys did not help clean up?
6. Why do you think the teacher (Mrs. Linkous) let them sit and read the story without telling them to help clean up?
7. Role play the situation.

Children should be helped to understand that two sides exist to every "moral" problem and that the needs of the individuals on each side of the problem should be considered. The solution to the problem should not come through immature behavior, such as the suggestion of the child to put the fingerpaint back on the table, but through deciding what is best for the entire group. The children should be led to discuss "respect" and understanding for how individuals feel on "both sides." Children have difficulty handling problems in which there is no definite

It was nearly time for a snack, and the teacher at the nursery school told the children it was time to clean up. The children worked very hard cleaning up the tables where they were finger-painting. They washed the floor around the tables where the paint had spilled. They took off

their aprons and went to the bathroom to wash their hands. Everyone in the room helped clean up except John and Jay and Mrs. Linkous. They were busy reading a book in the corner and did not even notice that it was nearly time for snack.

"It's not fair," said one of the children. "John and Jay did not have to help clean up, and we did."

"We don't want to clean up," responded John and Jay. "We are reading a story with Mrs. Linkous, and we're not finished."

"Teacher," shouted the other children, "they won't help clean up."

"Children," replied the teacher, "We already have the table cleaned up. John and Jay will have a turn next time."

"I'm going to put my fingerpaint back on the table so they will have something to clean up," shouted Keith.

"Let's all sit down and talk about this," replied the teacher. "Let's pretend *you* were reading a book, and the other children were cleaning up. What would you like to do? What do you think would be right?"

right or wrong; yet these kinds of problems help children develop moral maturity.

8
KINDNESS
VERSUS
CRUELTY

In considering goals for children, most people would list kindness and consideration rather than cruelty and thoughtlessness. How do we go about promoting kindness? Is kindness natural, or is cruelty to be expected in a young child?

In studying the development of young children and in observing their behavior, we often see a young child not considering the needs of another. As we have mentioned, a young child is egocentric and sees the world from his point of view rather than from the point of view of another. What may seem cruel to others may not seem cruel to young children as they attempt to fulfill their needs. During the stage of toddlerhood (ages 1½ to three years), adults see interactions between children as rough and physical. If a toddler wants someone else's toy, instead of courteously asking for it, she grabs, pushes, hits, or bites to get what she wants. Some children are much more aggressive than others, as most preschool teachers and parents can verify, but the point is that physical aggression during toddlerhood is typical and quite normal. Children at this young age do not treat other children as "they would like to be treated" because basically they lack empathy. Often they treat other people like toys or inanimate objects to be pushed and tossed around. As a child progresses into the preschool years, he or she has more ability to understand other people's feelings and to treat them personally rather than as inanimate objects.

If rough and inconsiderate behavior is typical of young children, should this behavior be accepted as normal? Should nothing be done to change it? It *can* be changed. Help children find preferable ways of interacting with others; help them see that kindness works better than cruelty.

Before discussing how we help children become kind and considerate, let us discuss what cruelty is and discover some possible reasons children have for behaving cruelly.

Cruelty is enjoying the pain, discomfort, misfortune, or grief of another person. A cruel child enjoys, either emotionally or physically, hurting others. In using this definition then, we could not say that a toddler is cruel when he interacts with other children in a rough and physical aggressive manner. This may be the only way he knows how to get what he wants, but he doesn't respond this way because he enjoys seeing others hurt. However, his behavior may *lead* to cruel behavior if parents and teachers do not act in some way to help him see when he hurts others.

Listed below are some possible reasons for cruel behavior of children:

1. To *counterhurt*—often children have been hurt either emotionally or physically, and their response often is to counterhurt. Most of the time they do not hurt the person who hurt them, but they direct their hurt toward whoever happens to be around and vulnerable. The example of the father yelling at the mother, the mother yelling at the child, and the child kicking the dog is a typical example of counterhurt. As we grow older, the counterhurt often takes the form of sarcasm or criticism. Young children, however, counterhurt more often with physical aggression, such as hitting, pushing, kicking, and biting, and verbal aggression, such as namecalling and arguing.

2. *Egocentricity,* or lack of awareness that they are really hurting another person. This would not be considered cruelty if we accepted the above definition, but often children respond in such a way that appears to be cruel to others when the motivation behind the act is not the enjoyment of others' pain, but simply a desire to fulfill one's own needs without considering the needs or feelings of another individual. Note how preschool boys will often run a truck or a car over a smaller person's arm or hand, seemingly not aware of the irritation caused to another.

3. *Not enough relationships with others.* Often children respond with cruelty because they do not know how to relate to others and are deficient in social interaction and relationships with others. They often act cruelly to gain attention, or in an attempt to make friends. A good example is a child in our preschool program named Teddy.

TEDDY AND THE PINCHING GAME   Teddy was always pinching other children. The other children hated to be pinched because it hurt. They would yell at

Teddy and try to avoid him whenever possible. Children would not sit by Teddy during story time because he would pinch them and make them cry. Teddy seemed to enjoy watching others cry. The teachers were disturbed by this behavior and decided to try some behavior modification techniques to stop Teddy's pinching.

First the teachers decided to ignore Teddy when he pinched the children and give him a lot of attention when he was behaving appropriately. The reasoning behind this technique was that Teddy appeared to be pinching other children to get their attention, and when that attention and reinforcement was withdrawn, the pinching should stop. The behavior modification attempt did not work, however, and the pinching continued.

The teachers reexamined the problem and decided that it was not the teacher's attention Teddy was seeking but other children's attention. He was trying in his own way to establish a relationship with other children, and did not seem to know how.

Now the behavior modification project changed, and the teachers tried to reinforce Teddy when he was interacting with other children in an appropriate way by saying such things as "It's nice to have friends," or "Jay likes it when you play blocks with him," or "Isn't it fun to fingerpaint with your friends." When Teddy started the pinching, he was immediately taken from the group. A teacher then sat and talked to him about how good friends don't pinch each other but do nice things with each other, explaining how it hurts to be pinched and that other children do not like it. She then asked Teddy to name some things he could do with his friends that would not hurt them.

After several weeks Teddy stopped the pinching. Eventually he learned some alternative ways of relating to other children without hurting them.

4. *Dominance*: Another possible reason for cruelty is that some children want to dominate and be in charge. One way they can do this is by being cruel and by hurting others. These children's feelings of adequacy and competence seem to be lacking, and they feel the need to dominate always. The following story is another true story of a child in one of our preschool programs:

Kelly was a cute little brown-haired boy with big brown laughing eyes. He always had a smile on his face and seemed to enjoy life. Kelly had a problem with other boys and girls, how-

THE LITTLE BOSS

89

ever. He liked to be mean to them. The children liked Kelly when he was nice, but when he was mean, they were afraid and stayed away from him. Some of the mean things Kelly did to the other children included things like throwing sand in their eyes, hitting them on the head with blocks, locking the girls up in the animal cages, riding the tricycle the wrong way and crashing into other children on trikes, taking toys away, knocking over block buildings, running over fingers with play trucks, pushing children out of swings, tearing books, pushing learning materials on the floor, and so on.

Each day when Kelly came to school, he would always go to the first table he saw and knock everything onto the floor. That upset the teachers. Then he would go into the housekeeping area where the girls were, take the dolls away from the children, throw them into the sink, turn on the water, and drown them. After the dolls were drowned, Kelly would gather them all up and throw them into the garbage. The garbage was a big tall can; so the teacher had to get the dolls out. The girls cried and cried, but Kelly was happy.

After Kelly had thrown the dolls into the garbage, he would go over to the table where the children were painting on big sheets of paper with easel paint. "Would you like to paint?" the teacher would ask Kelly.

"I guess so," said Kelly. He dipped his paint brush into some bright blue paint and then got an idea. "Look teacher," shouted Kelly. The teacher turned around and looked, and Kelly flipped the paint brush into her face. Bright blue paint covered the teacher's face.

"Kelly," she shouted, "I want you to sit on this chair while I wash my face off." While the teacher went to wash her face and to tell another teacher to watch Kelly, he ran quickly over to the block area where a table was set up containing rice and measuring cups for the children to pour and measure. Kelly started pouring the rice all over the floor. When he saw a teacher coming, he ran over to the other side of the block area and knocked down a tower that one of the children was building. The teacher finally "captured" him and had to isolate him for a long time until he could settle down.

"Kelly," she said, "I can't let you do all these bad things. It makes other people feel bad." Kelly smiled.

"Do you like to be the boss, Kelly?"

"Yes," said Kelly. "I like to be the boss."

"Then how about being the kind of boss that other people like?" the teacher said. "Let's try to think of some ways." The teacher and Kelly talked about some ways that he could be a good boss that everyone liked instead of a bad boss that everyone was afraid of.

*   *   *   *   *

Later, with a teacher sticking pretty close to Kelly's side most of the day, anticipating his behavior and watching for his build-ups, and with the use of some behavior modification techniques, Kelly began to become less cruel, his behavior more appropriate. His case is a classic example of dominance. Fortunately, most teachers do not see such extreme behavior. Children like Kelly must have their behavior evaluated and must be told how it affects others around them. They need to be helped to see alternatives to their cruel behavior and to gain feelings of empathy for the children they are behaving cruelly toward. Kelly was a classic example of a manipulator as well, because whenever the teacher would become angry with him, he would charm her until she no longer felt angry. He also charmed the other children into doing almost anything he wanted.

In examining the motives behind his behavior, we determined that his sole motive was to dominate and to have power over others. Along with his desire for power was a desire for attention. He loved to have the teachers angry at him. He was literally the *Little Boss*!

5. *Lack of responsibility for the feelings of others.* As we discussed earlier, at a young age children have difficulty understanding the feelings of others. A child may not understand why mother gets so upset and cries when she walks on her newly shampooed carpet with muddy feet. The little girl doesn't understand why her teacher is angry and upset when she walks in the bathroom and sees water running on the floor. After all, the children had a good time when they were splashing it. Unless adults call the child's attention to the needs of others, and help the child see that she must assume some responsibility for the feelings of others, she will continue to be insensitive to their needs and feelings. Parents and teachers both need to show respect for children and expect respect from children; expect them to be responsible for the feelings of those around them.

How do children become kind and how do parents help the egocentric child move from thinking only about self to thinking about others and their needs?

1. *Kindness is rewarded.* Often children are reinforced for kindness from adults around them. As he or she grows older, the child becomes self-reinforcing and continues to behave in a

Reasons for Kindness

91

kind way toward other people. For example, while one of the authors was growing up, she was constantly told by her mother that she was the "family peacemaker" because of the kind of things she did for her brothers and sisters and because she was always trying to solve family conflicts and problems. Eventually she began to see herself as a peacemaker, a role that generalized into other relationships.

2. *Association.* As we become socialized, we associate certain feelings with positive or negative events. For example, we learn to associate negativism, fighting, and crime with unpleasant feelings and experiences. On the other hand, we learn to associate smiling, laughter, and kindness with positive and pleasant feelings and experiences. We learn to value those things that make us feel positive and happy. If teachers and parents want to help children engage in kind acts, they should structure the environment so that most of the time the child develops a positive feeling when he or she engages in kind and considerate acts. Similarly, when a child is engaging in cruel and inconsiderate acts, the environment should be structured in such a way that the child does not feel happy, but has unpleasant feelings.

Parents and teachers should be careful not to use excessive punishment or guilt-oriented techniques in trying to modify a child's cruel or inconsiderate behavior. In doing so, they are likely to arouse other negative behaviors, and the problem will not be solved. When an adult tries to help the child see that kind acts will bring better results and more positive feelings than cruel or unkind acts, the child will eventually learn that the world will be a happier place if he engages in kind and considerate behavior. Unfortunately, many parents and teachers make cruel and inconsiderate behavior rewarding by the way they respond to the child. Adults should carefully examine their response to a child's inappropriate behavior to see if they are not actually reinforcing the behavior they want to discourage.

3. *Altruism.* As children learn to *identify* with others, they find they are happy when another person is happy and sad when the other person is sad. In this case, the child attempts to relieve his sadness by relieving the other person's sadness, therefore attending to the needs of the other person. For example, if mother is sad because of the muddy footprints on the carpet, the child is also sad. To relieve the sadness of both mother and self, the child must do something. He tells mother he will help her clean up the carpet and that he is very sorry for making such a bad mess. Mother then wipes away the tears and smiles and says, "Okay, let's get out the sponge."

92

4. *Norm expectation.* Often children develop kind behavior because it is expected. "In this classroom we care about each other and will do nice things for each other." Such an expectation, especially if some members of the class respond, will likely get results. Adults must be careful not to tell the child how he *should* feel but simply develop a behavioral expectation of kindness. Perhaps at first the child does not feel happy doing the dishes for his brother, but as this act becomes associated with positive feelings and responses and is an expected norm, eventually the child will be performing kind acts because he wants to and because they make him happy. Teachers can set up norm expectation in the classroom in developing kindness. Expectations such as helping other children pick up the blocks or clean up the tables or helping a child button buttons are acts that can be expected and reinforced at the same time.

5. *Modeling.* Parents and teachers who model kind and considerate behavior are more likely to influence the child to exhibit kind and considerate behavior. Adults should, however, expect the same behavior from the child, so that the adult doesn't give everything and the child nothing.

Discussion Questions:

1. Why did Dallas take the money?
2. How did Shane feel?
3. Was it a funny joke to take the money?
4. Is it okay to play mean jokes on people?
5. Is it okay to take people's money if you give it back?
6. Was Shane happy to get his birthday money? How did he feel after it had been taken?
7. What should the mom and dad have done?
8. Should Shane take Dallas' money?
9. Should Dallas take Shane's money again and play another joke on him?

Additional ideas to use with the same story format:

1. Hiding lunch tickets at school.
2. Hiding a new toy.
3. Hiding a "just purchased" treat.
4. Hiding new shoes.
5. Hiding the baby's blanket.

Shane just had a birthday. His grandmother had sent him a five-dollar bill, and he was proud of having so much money. Also, his friend had given him a dollar; even his aunt Carma had given him a dollar. He was seven dollars rich now, and happy. Shane left his money and all his presents on his bed and ran out of his room. His brother Dallas went into the room and saw the money. Dallas thought it would be funny to hide the money so Shane couldn't find it. So Dallas hid the money.

While Shane was playing, Dallas went to Cub Scout meeting and forgot to get Shane's money out of the hiding place. Later Shane went into his room to look at all his presents and saw that his money was gone. "Where's my money?" cried Shane. "Somebody took it."

"It must be here somewhere," said mother. "Maybe it dropped off the bed." They looked everywhere. They looked on top of the bed, under the bed, and everywhere, but there was no money. They even looked under the covers, but there was no money. They looked under and beside the bed, but there was no money. They looked under the dresser, in Shane's pockets, in the closets, on the table, in Shane's new birthday toys, under the couch, by the birthday cake, and even in Shane's shoes, but they could not find Shane's money.

Shane was very sad. "Now my money is gone and I am not rich any more. I know somebody

94

took it. Did you take it, Randy?" "No," said Randy. "Did you take it, Allen?" "No," said Allen, "Did you take it Mom and Dad?" "No," said Mom and Dad. "Well, then it must have been Dallas," said Shane.

When Dallas came home Shane asked him, "Did you take my money, Dallas?" "Yes," said Dallas. "Wasn't that a funny joke?" Nobody laughed. Dallas went to his room and got the money. "I'm going to take your money now," said Shane.

Discussion Questions:
1. What did the girls do?
2. Why did they play the joke on the family?
3. Was it a good thing to do?
4. How did the family feel?
5. How did the girls feel?
6. Did the girls do the right thing in giving the money back?
7. Did giving the money back make the joke okay?
8. What do you think the grandma would do when she found out?

Karen and Marilyn went to grandma's house to visit for two weeks. They loved to go to grandma's house because there were so many fun things to do. Grandma lived out on a farm; so there were the tractors to drive, the wheat bin to get into, the hay stack to climb, and the barns to play house in. As the girls were playing quietly in the bedroom while grandma took a nap, they found an old candy box. "Let's make some mud candy and give it to the Wilson children across the street," said Marilyn. "Okay," said Karen. "We can even charge them for it so we can make some money."

The girls went outside and found a nice big pile of mud. They rolled ten balls of mud to look like candy. Then they took the candy next door. "Would you like to buy some chocolate candy? It's only fifty cents," said Karen to Alice Wilson.

"I'll go ask mother," said Alice and she ran in the house to get her mother. Mother came out of the house followed by the whole family. They all looked very eager to buy the candy. The family was poor, and they had to search all over the house for some money but finally found enough to buy the candy.

Karen and Marilyn looked at each other with a scared look. "What are we going to do?" whispered Marilyn. Mother Wilson paid the girls for the candy. They took the money and ran as fast as they could and hid in the barn. "What is

96

Grandma going to say when she finds out?" asked Marilyn.

Meanwhile, the Wilson family had all gathered around to eat what they thought was some nice chocolate candy. When they opened the box and saw the mud balls, they were all very disappointed. "Those girls tricked us," they said.

Karen and Marilyn started feeling bad, so they returned the money to the Wilson family, who were glad to get the money back. But they were still disappointed that they didn't get the candy they were planning on. The girls felt bad that they had played the trick on the family, and they apologized.

9
SHARING
VERSUS
SELFISHNESS

Most adults want children to share instead of being selfish. Sharing, however, is not easy for a young child. He does not understand that the other child wants something as much as he does and tends to think of his own feelings first. As the child grows older and is able to understand the needs and feelings of others, he will have an easier time sharing. The young child, however, must first develop the feeling of "mine" in order to share later. One of the authors had a representative experience in a headstart setting when scissors were passed out to the children. One child grabbed all the scissors and held them close to her chest and said, "Mine, they are all mine. I'm going to keep them all." This child had very likely not had the experience of having something of her very own that she could call hers. She knew that she couldn't use all the scissors; nevertheless, she wanted them all. I talked with her and helped her see the needs of the other children by saying, "Regina, the other boys and girls want to cut, and they don't have anything to cut with. What do you think we should do?" After I had helped her see the needs of others and told her the rule is that right now each child can only have one pair of scissors, Regina carefully handed a pair of scissors to each child.

Can young children learn to share? What can an adult do to help a child learn to share? Why do some people become more selfish as they grow older and never learn to share? Let us look first at reasons for selfishness developing.

1. *Not having a capacity to be aware.* This is an egocentric stage of development and is not considered real selfishness but is self-centeredness. A good example of this is when a young child goes to a birthday party and takes a present. When he gets there, he decides the present is his and does not want to give it

or even share it with the child who is having a birthday. Because of his stage of development, he does not have the capacity to be aware that other people want things just as much as he does. When this young child sees that the birthday child has all the gifts, he thinks it only fair that he should keep the present he brought. He forgets that on his birthday he received all the presents.

2. *Switching off feelings for others.* Responding to the needs and feelings of others starts very early in a child's life. Take the example of the young baby who reaches up and claws his mother's face. The baby does not understand that clawing mother's face will hurt Mother. If Mother laughs and reinforces this behavior, it will continue. If, however, she firmly takes the baby's hand and says "No, no. That hurts Mommy's face—It makes Mommy cry (exhibit fake cry) when you scratch her face." The baby will soon learn that mommy has feelings and that his or her behavior can have an effect on mommy's feelings. The child then develops feelings similar to those of the adults because of the identification process, and when mommy feels sad, the child feels sad. As the child continues to have more of these experiences in which the adult or another child lets the child know of how his or her behavior affects their feelings, the child will learn to control and inhibit some behaviors because it hurts the feelings of another person and also hurts the emotions of the child.

Sometimes after children have learned that their behavior influences the feelings of others as well as their own feelings, they *switch off* these feelings for others and become centered on self. This "switch off" often occurs during the adolescent years, but sometimes before. It is as if the child learns that it hurts him to carry and feel other people's emotional burdens. By learning to ignore this extra emotional baggage, he avoids the unpleasantness and has more time to look after his own needs. The teacher or mother of such a child is constantly in a turmoil and asks the child to do something, giving the child the impression that he must perform to help relieve the adult's stress. Soon the child realizes that no matter what he does, such a teacher or parent will always be in some kind of distress. Isn't it easier simply to tune out the siren of the fire truck than constantly to pour glasses of water on the fire? The child realizes it is hopeless to provide constant and adequate emotional comfort. He learns to be insensitive to the constant barrage of distress signals from the adult.

3. *Prevailing Norm.* The norm for some children may be that they expect to have their work done for them. They do not feel

selfish because they have learned that being waited upon is a norm or rule. Certainly children from the old nobility and the royal families were taught that others existed to provide them pleasure. This happens even today. As an example, consider the case of a boy raised by a doting grandmother, who did everything for him: served his meals the way he wanted them to be served, cleaned up his table and his dishes, brought glasses of water and soft drinks to him while he was watching television, and did all household and personal maintenance, expecting nothing in return. As this boy grew older, he expected the same service from other people and did not sense this expectation as selfishness.

On the other hand, some homes have a prevailing norm of not sharing. No one shares money or treats. At Christmas each child very carefully guards his stocking so that no one will take anything. If one child brings home a large bottle of soft drink from the movie, he will not give any to his siblings even though he is full of the drink—because he does not want to share. In this family sharing is something that simply is not taught. This norm can continue as a way of life.

In other homes a more simple but extreme focus exists on the self—how one looks, how one can look *better* than the other children in the class, how one can have more or better things (clothes, toys, club memberships) than friends or siblings. In this home the norm is selfishness. The result is similar to having a norm of not sharing.

4. *Valuing other things as more important than relationships with people*: This child learns to value things more than people. She is more concerned about how she is dressed than how she relates to other people. Thus, when this person must choose between a material tangible benefit and a personal relationship, the possession is stronger. Jim, coming from a very poor family, may be as kind and considerate as Richard until material possessions are involved. Then he becomes excited about a new toy, and he appears selfish. Jim might be more inclined to let Richard choose a television show than Richard would be to let Jim do so. However, when *possessions* are the issue, Jim is definitely more selfish. Here we have too much emphasis on material possessions.

How, then, can we train young children to share?

1. *Understand the development of the child* and do not place expectations on him too far above his developmental level. Insisting that children share at a young age can only complicate the

problem. As we stated before, the child has to have his own possessions before he can learn to share.

2. *Help the young child have something of his own* that no one is allowed to touch. Everyone needs his own personal space and personal things. Children, like adults, should not be expected to share everything. Give children boxes that they can decorate and put their "special things" in. They need a locker at school (or a box or a can or a cubby) of their very own. At home they need some drawers that are theirs and a bed and a special place in the bedroom for their own things. Children who are not allowed to have their own things often grow up feeling frustrated and always wanting things. Having something for self helps children give more in the long run. However, children should simultaneously be learning the benefits of sharing their possession with others.

3. *Help children understand the needs of others* by telling stories and discussing the needs of the characters in a story and by pointing out examples in real life. For example, when two children are fighting over a toy truck and both children refuse to share, the teacher can point out that both children want the truck very much and it makes them sad not to be able to play with it, but the teacher wants to be fair to both children; so she will have to put the truck up until the next day when they can try to work out the problem.

Another story tells of one child who has a large pile of play dough, and another child wants to play with it. The child with all the play dough should be helped to see that the other child would also like to play, but he doesn't have any play dough. The teacher can try to help the first child "feel" that if he didn't have any play dough, he would be sad. But if the other child shared with him, he would be happy.

4. *Role Playing* is a good method of helping a child understand the feelings of others and of helping him learn to share. One proven role-playing technique is to bring two children in front of the group and give one child two toys, the other none. The teacher tells the children that the child with no toys has just come over to the other child's house to play, but she doesn't have any toys to play with; the other child has two toys. The teacher asks the child with two toys what she would do. In every case the child with the two toys gives one toy to the other child. The teacher then says a lot of reinforcing things, such as, "Isn't it nice to share? It was so nice of you to give the other child a toy. You are a good friend to have." Both children feel good.

Two other children are now given a chance to do the very same thing until each child in the group has been given a chance to role-play sharing. The children never tire of the "sharing game" and want to play it over and over again.

Teachers must be careful not to punish or ridicule a child who does not give a toy to the other child. The teacher should *not* tell the child what he *should* do, but should let him discover it on his own. By watching the other children sharing and being reinforced for sharing, the child will later learn that sharing is a good thing.

Some children will do the opposite of what is expected for attention-getting purposes. For this reason as well, teachers need to be careful not to pay too much attention to such a response. They could say something like, "I see you have chosen a different way of handling the problem." No more needs to be said. The teacher should then give two more children a chance to act out the role.

5. The above discussion of role playing also includes using *reinforcement* when the child exhibits the desired behavior (sharing). Teachers and parents need to be aware of sharing behavior that occurs during the day, reinforcing the unselfish act with a *pat on the child's back* or *words* of *praise* such as, "It's nice to share," or "I like the way you two are sharing the blocks today. It's more fun when two are working together," or "Thank you for sharing your cookie with me, Darin. I like cookies," or "It must make you happy to share the dress-up clothes. I can tell you are having more fun today than you were yesterday." When a teacher expresses praise and encouragement, children eventually began to say the same things to themselves, "Yes, I *am* happy to share the dress-up clothes. It *is* more fun to share."

Occasionally parents can use material rewards as well, but care should be used. Rewards often become bribes, which do not teach mature moral behavior. The following incident is an example of how material rewards might be used effectively. Two hungry boys have shared a package of french fries without fighting or fussing. The adult says, "I appreciate the way you boys shared the french fries. You deserve another package."

6. Parents and teachers who *model* sharing behavior rather than selfishness are more likely to be influential in helping children develop this type of behavior. Respect is an essential part of making modeling work. The adult must respect the child and must also expect the child to respect the adult. An adult who shares and gives everything but expects nothing in return is not teaching the child to share but to be selfish.

STORY # 1
SHARING
LEGOS

Questions:
1. How did Justin feel?
2. How did the other children feel?
3. Who wanted the legos?
4. Why didn't Justin want to share?
5. What do you think the teacher should have said?

The teacher brought out the big box of legos. The children were excited because they loved to play with the legos. When the teacher put the box on the table, Justin started grabbing all the legos for himself.

"I want all these," said Justin.

"But we have to share with all the children," said the teacher.

"No," said Justin. "I need all of these or I can't build the tower I want to build."

"You can't have them all," shouted the children.

104

Richard came over to Kevin's house to play. "You can't play with any of my toys," said Kevin. "You always break them."

Richard was sad. He liked Kevin's big airplane and wanted to play with that. "You better let me play with your toys, or I'll go home and never come back again," said Richard. "I let you play with my toys when you come to my house."

"But I don't break your toys. You break my toys. I'm not going to share," said Kevin.

Richard was sad and walked away. "I guess I will go home then," said Richard.

STORY #2
SHARING
TOYS

Discussion Questions:
1. What happened?
2. Which boy wouldn't share?
3. Which boy was sad?
4. Why wouldn't Kevin share?
5. Do you think it is good to share?
6. Was it good or bad for Kevin not to share?
7. Would you share your toys with Richard if you were Kevin?

10
COOPERATION VERSUS FIGHTING

If the question "What is your major problem with children?" were asked teachers and parents, they would probably answer, "*Fighting!*" On the other hand, if they were asked "What is one of the most important goals for children?" they would probably reply, "Cooperation." Cooperation involves sharing, kindness, empathy, respect, understanding rules, and delaying gratification. A child who is able to cooperate (which is more than simply obeying) is really a joy to have in a classroom or a family. Children refusing to cooperate make the job of a parent or a teacher much more difficult. In addition, to be successful in adult life, children must learn to cooperate.

To understand more about cooperation, let's begin by understanding fighting. Why do children (and older people) fight? In many cases fighting is a form of communication. First, there are many kinds of fighting. We see young children "jostling" and having a great time doing so. This is more of a physical exercise and usually does not involve feelings of hostility or anger. There are other types of fighting, however, that are physically and emotionally damaging to the child as well as extremely irritating to adults. Ask most teachers, and they will tell you that the incessant in-class fighting between two or more children is almost intolerable. To help parents and teachers understand this intolerable situation, we have listed possible explanations of why children fight.

Nearly everyone fights in one way or another. Rudolf Dreikurs, in the book *Children the Challenge* (1964, p. 201), discusses the subject:

Most parents feel deep concern about the endless fighting that goes on among brothers and sisters. They love each child, and it hurts to see those

**Fighting Is A
Part of Life**

107

one loves hate and hurt each other. A great deal of child-raising energy goes into settling fights and trying to "teach" the children to get along together. Many children eventually "outgrow" fighting and begin to appreciate and care for each other as they grow up. Others continue the hostility into adulthood and never make peace with their siblings. No amount of preaching seems to ease the friction. It keeps on popping up. Most parents have tried every known procedure for stopping fights—and still they continue. Fighting among siblings is so common that it has become accepted as a "normal" form of child behavior. It is not normal just because it occurs so regularly. Children do not have *to fight. Homes where children do not fight are possible. When they fight, there is something wrong in the relationships. No one can honestly feel good while fighting. Therefore, if children continue to fight, they must be able to gain satisfaction, not so much in the fight as in the results.*

While many people excuse fighting as "normal," we feel that in *excess* it is directly connected with other problems.

Fighting Is A Form of Communication

Especially for young children, fighting is one of the ways in which they communicate. Because they have not learned other more efficient and desirable forms of communication, the young toddler will fight to get what he wants and to influence others.

Fighting Is Expected

Often children are expected to fight. Boys, at a very young age in particular, are taught by their dads to "fight it out" and not let the other guy "get away with that."

Fighting Is Attention Getting

Children fight to gain the attention of mother or teacher. The reaction on the part of the adult is usually one of irritation or annoyance, as in the following illustration:

Mother was talking on the telephone. Jani and Heather were playing with the paper dolls. "That's mine," shouted Heather, taking away one of the paper dolls. "No, it isn't, it's mine," shouted Jani. The girls fought and fought over the paper doll until it was torn. Jani started to cry, and Heather started yelling, "It's all your fault. You tore the paper doll, and it was mine."

Mother put the phone down on her shoulder and shouted, "Girls, stop fighting. Can't you see I'm talking on the telephone?" The girls continued to argue over who had torn the doll and whose it was until finally mother got off the phone and gave them both spankings.

It appears from this illustration that not only were the girls frustrated about the paper doll and about tearing it, but they

108

were also trying to seek the attention of their mother. Mother, of course, gave them attention.

Often because they do not know any other way to take out their frustration, children act aggressively and fight with other children. Often the source of the frustration is caused by a lack of satisfaction of physical needs (not enough sleep, food, warmth), or frustration caused by the lack of ability to complete a task successfully, or frustration caused by a lack of satisfaction of emotional, creative, or intellectual needs, as illustrated in the following incidents.

Children Fight Because of Frustration

- Two-year-old Sue could not get the square block in the square hole, so she got mad and threw the box of blocks at her sister. Her sister hit her back because the box hurt her, and Sue hit her sister back because she had hurt Sue when she hit her. Pretty soon both girls were screaming and crying.
- Four-year-old Jeff was trying to put a puzzle together. He could not get the pieces to fit, so he threw the puzzle on the floor. "You shouldn't do that," said Harold. "You're dumb." "I am not," said Jeff, and he hit Harold. Harold hit Jeff back, and pretty soon both boys were fighting.
- Andy had just awakened from his nap and was still tired. As he was putting his shoes on, one of his friends said, "Andy's awake." Andy got mad and started to hit his friend, and soon the boys were fighting.

A tremendous amount of research has been conducted on modeling aggressive behavior. Children do act more aggressively after watching an aggressive model. The theory is that children will fight more if their parents fight and argue with each other. Also, children tend to fight more after viewing television in which aggression is displayed in cartoon form as well as real dramas.

Children Fight Because of Modeling

Parents and teachers who allow fighting to occur are usually encouraging more fighting. This idea might be in contrast to the theory that children fight for attention, and if the adult pays that attention, the fighting will continue. The important thing to remember is *not to take sides in the fight.* It is almost impossible to know all the details of a fight; therefore, adults should treat children as a group. For example, the teacher might say to two boys who are fighting over a truck, "I can see that you boys are not willing to work things out with the truck. I'll have to put it up on the shelf. Maybe you can try again

Children Fight Because of Permissiveness

109

tomorrow." The teacher did not try to figure out which boy had the truck first, and therefore did not take sides.

Another statement the adult could make is "I'm sorry you two are having trouble over the paper dolls, but I'm sure you can work it out between you."

When the fighting gets too rough, and either Mother or teacher feels it should be stopped, she should treat the children as a group. "You will both need to come in now since you can't play together in the sandbox," or "You boys can choose to stop fighting or go to bed," or "You'll have to stop fighting now. You can each go to your rooms to calm down a bit."

Usually the children are happy that the teacher sets some limits and does not allow the fighting to continue—especially the child who is getting hurt.

Children Fight Because of a Desire for Power

According to Dreikurs:

There is always a power contest involved in a fight. Equals don't need to use conflicts as an opportunity to gain superiority. They can resolve the differences without victory or defeat. But when one's feeling of status is threatened by the move of another, the conflict becomes a contest. Hostility is aroused to justify disregard for politeness and consideration, and one seeks to restore his supposed loss of status at the expense of his opponent. When we side with the baby, protect the youngest against the oldest, stand up for the seemingly "abused" one, then we strengthen his feeling of inferiority and teach the victim how to use deficiency and weakness to gain special consideration; thus augmenting the very feeling that needs to be eliminated."

Dreikurs feels that children, when left to their own devices, establish far more equal and just relationships than adults can provide. "Children will learn, by the impact of reality, to develop diplomacy, equality, fair play, justice, consideration, and respect for each other." (Dreikurs, 1964, pp. 213–14.)

TEACHING CHILDREN NOT TO FIGHT

What can parents and teachers do, then, to teach children not to fight?

● Dreikurs says to "*stay out of children's fights.*" By doing so, we allow children the learning experience of trying to "work things out on their own." As we stated above, children learn to be just, fair, considerate, and respectful of each other. They also learn that fighting is not the way to get an adult's attention. Sometimes even exceptional children behave so cruelly toward smaller children that both compassion and a sense of fairness dictate intervention. In these cases, physical separation of the two children is probably the most successful solution.

110

• *Teach alternate responses.* When children are frustrated, they need to draw from responses other than aggression that cope with their frustration. Children should not be taught to "ignore" their feelings of frustration by pretending they do not exist, but they do need to learn alternate actions. One alternative to physical aggression is emotional aggression, which will hopefully turn out to be a healthy confrontation. Children need to express their frustrations in a healthy way by using verbalization with strong emotion, if necessary. Here's an example:

Angela finger painted a pretty picture at the table where she was working. Rusty, sitting next to Angela, messed up her picture. Angela became so angry she began beating her hands on the table, splashing finger paint all over Rusty's face. "What's going on?" asked the teacher.

"Rusty messed up my picture," cried Angela, "and now it is all ruined."

The teacher wanted to help the children see that fighting was not the way to solve the problem. "Angela, can you think of a better way to let Rusty know you didn't like what he did to your picture?"

"No," said Angela. "I just don't like him any more. He ruined my picture."

The teacher persisted. "Angela, can you think of a way to *tell* Rusty you didn't like what he did without splashing paint all over him?"

"I guess so," said Angela. "I don't like what you did to my picture, Rusty. I worked really hard on it and now it's all ruined. Would you like somebody to do that to your picture?"

"No," said Rusty shamefully. "I'm sorry, Angela. I didn't mean to make you sad. I just wanted some of your finger paint."

"Will you promise not to do it again?" asked Angela forgivingly.

"Yes, I promise. I won't mess your picture up again," said Rusty.

"There now," said the teacher. "Wasn't that a better way than fighting?"

Another method of teaching alternate responses is to help children find constructive outlets for their aggressive behavior. Teachers and parents can show children how to use positive alternatives such as the following:

· "You can hammer the nail in the wood, but I can't let you hit people's toes."

· "You can dance to the music, but I can't let you push the other children."

- "You can build with the blocks, but I can't let you hit Billy on the head with them."
- "Show me how you can paint with the paint brush. Those are such pretty colors." (The child is annoying children who are painting.)
- "Show me how fast you can run. You are such a good runner. Let's go outside." (The child is running into children who are working on other projects.)

Another alternate response that should be encouraged is cooperation. Children should be encouraged to see that because of cooperation two can be happy rather than one happy and one sad. When children cooperate, no one loses and everyone gains. As an example, two children are building with Legos, but neither child has enough Legos to build a big tower. If, however, they work together and build the tower as a team, they not only have enough Legos to build the tower, but they have a good time building it. The experience becomes not only physically and intellectually stimulating and creative but socializing as well.

● *Help children understand that life is not always fair.* Even though we would like it to be, life is not always fair, and we can't guarantee a just and fair environment. It is impossible, for example, for parents to treat children in a family equally at all times, just as it is impossible for teachers to treat children in the classroom equally at all times. Often children do something wrong and do not get punished. Other children see the situation as unfair and attempt to "take things into their own hands." It should be explained to children that this is not their responsibility. Consider, for example, a child who broke the convertible top on the family car by turning on the switch when the top was fastened. "I'm going to beat him up," said his brother. "Now we can't put down the top until we get it fixed." Mother quietly reminds the protesting boy that she will take care of it.

Life is not always fair at school. Some children get more cake in the lunch line than another child, or more candy at a class party. Some teachers let the same children hold the pictures up all the time, or help her with the table setting. Some children are not allowed to do things when other children are. Children should be reminded that adults are trying their best to make things fair; but when they don't, a child should express his opinion to the adult rather than fight with the privileged child.

● *Give children a place to direct their grievances.* The basis of democracy is that everyone deserves the right to respect and dignity, and everyone deserves the right to be heard. This is the basis of a law-abiding environment. Children should assist in developing a place and time when their grievances can be heard and judged fairly. In families this should take the form of a family council. At school it could take the form of a "talking time." It should be carefully set up so that it does not involve too many people, especially when young children are concerned. Young children can become overwhelmed with other people's complaints and grievances; these can start arguments, which compound their problems. Probably no more than two or three young children in a classroom should be involved.

In a family, all members could be involved, but the parents must control the discussion to keep the feelings positive, rational, and objective. When children learn that their grievances will be listened to and dealt with, they are less likely to fight with each other in order to solve the problem. The children in the family council or the "school talking time" are encouraged to think of creative suggestions to the problem, and the adult should be willing to go along with the group's suggestions.

For example, one family had a problem with fighting over whose turn it was to do the dishes. The group members suggested that the job assignments should last for a week: washing dishes for a week, drying them for a week, and clearing the table for a week. The children tried it. It worked. Now this is the schedule the family follows.

Fighting over who was going to be first in the lunch line was a problem that came up in school. The teacher allowed the children to discuss the problem. They decided the quietest one should go first. "Fine," said the teacher. But when she tried to decide who was the quietest, she could not. They were all quiet. So the children had to think of another solution. "How about taking turns?" asked Bob. "Let each table take turns being first each day." The class tried this suggestion, and it worked.

• *Tell stories and present children with moral dilemmas in which children in the stories are trying to solve a problem.* Allow the children to solve the problem. Accept their ideas, and try to guide their comments to include a solution that would be fair to all the children involved.

• *Role play.* As we have stated in previous chapters, one of the most effective ways of helping children understand the feelings of another person is to ask them to play the role of the other. Do not allow the children to fight physically, but encourage them to try to solve the problem with other means (compromise, expression of feelings and expectations, confrontation, or cooperation).

• *Reinforce a child's attempts at solving problems and disputes without fighting.* Many children have already learned, either through their own experience and observation or through the efforts of a significant adult in their life, some very effective ways of handling and solving conflicts. The following are a few suggestions:

· *Confrontation.* The child stands up for his rights through the use of emotional, verbal, and rational means.

· *Mediation.* Work with an objective outsider, most often an adult, and allow him or her to decide how to solve the problem.

· *Compromise.* Neither party is totally satisfied with the solution to the problem, but both are willing to sacrifice to avoid conflict.

For example: Two children want all the clay dough or the blocks. Since neither child will be happy if one child has all the clay dough or the blocks, a compromise is that each child have an equal amount. Neither child is completely happy, but both children are happier than they would be without any clay dough or any blocks.

· *Cooperation.* A "no-lose" method, cooperation is usually a more satisfying solution than compromise because the children work together. In the above example, each child has half the clay dough or half the blocks. But if the children share and work together, they have more than they would apart. Socialization skills are thus developed.

· *Psychological manipulation.* A child who manipulates others could be called an "expeditor" or a "facilitator." Some adults reject this method used by some children, but it can be effective at times as training for a later occupation in life, such as a salesman.

The following true story is a good example of a child who is able to use psychological manipulation.

Mother had just picked up Shane from nursery school. It was a pretty day in October, and the leaves were just changing colors. "Mom, could we buy a pumpkin for Halloween?" Shane asked.

"No," said mother. "It's a whole month until Halloween. If we buy a pumpkin now, it will rot by Halloween."

Shane thought about that for a minute. "Then why do they have them at the fruit market already? Will they get rotten there before Halloween?"

"I guess not," said mother. "I suppose we could just buy one and keep it outside until Halloween. We are *not* going to carve a jack-o-lantern face, though, because if we cut the pumpkin

114

now, it really will get rotten by Halloween. Besides, I am very busy today and don't have time to help you." "Okay," said Shane. "I'm glad I can buy a pumpkin."

So mother and Shane stopped at the fruit market and found a big, round pumpkin. When they arrived home, Shane jumped out of the car. "Please help me carry the pumpkin to the front porch, Mommy," said Shane. "I just want to look at it. Thank you for buying such a pretty pumpkin."

Shane lay on his stomach on the front porch with his chin in his hands and looked at his pumpkin for a long time. He was talking to the pumpkin, but mother couldn't hear what he was saying. Then he got an idea. He ran to the dresser drawer and pulled out a black marking pen. "Mother," he said, "Could you just *draw* a jack-o-lantern face on my pumpkin with this marking pen?"

"Well, I guess so," said mother. "I guess it won't take long to draw a face." So mother drew some eyes and a nose and a big smiling mouth on the pumpkin.

"Thank you," said Shane. "My pumpkin looks really neat now." He plopped himself down on the porch again, put his chin in his hands, and looked at his pumpkin. He talked again to the pumpkin, but mother didn't hear what he was saying.

In a little while Shane came back into the house. "Mom, I just had an idea. Could you just cut a hole in the top of the pumpkin so I can scoop all the seeds and everything out?"

"I told you the pumpkin would rot by Halloween if we carved it today, Shane," said mother.

"But I want to scoop it out now, and if it gets rotten I could use my allowance to buy another pumpkin for Halloween," said Shane convincingly.

Mother thought to herself that it really wouldn't take a very long time to cut off the top of the pumpkin. And Shane was having such a good time. Besides, it would keep him busy for a while. So mother cut off the top of the pumpkin. It took her only a few minutes. "There now, Shane," mother said. "You take this big spoon and this newspaper and put all the seeds and the insides of the pumpkin on the newspaper."

Shane worked for a very long time scooping out the insides of the pumpkin. He worked for nearly two hours, then came running in to mother, shouting, "Come and see, Mother. Come and see what a good job I did." Mother walked out to the porch with Shane and saw that he had done a very good job on the insides of the pumpkin.

"What a nice job you did, Shane," mother said. "I'm proud of you."

"Mom, now that I have all the insides scooped out, do you think you could cut the eyes and nose and mouth? It won't take very long," said Shane pleadingly.

Mother looked at his big blue eyes and laughed. He surely did want to have that pumpkin made into a jack-o-lantern! So she said, "I guess so. You sure did have a good time today with your pumpkin, didn't you?"

"Yes, I did. I just love jack-o-lanterns. Thanks, Mom, for helping me."

This child very effectively used psychological manipulation rather than argument to get what he wanted. He was so charming and convincing that his mother didn't mind helping him. Shane was respectful of his mother's time and did not infringe too much at any one time. He was also reinforcing toward her so that she felt good about helping him. If this child continues to use this approach toward other people, he will probably be successful and well liked.

Psychological manipulation can be observed at times when young children have disputes with each other. Consider Reid and Jerry fighting over a piece of pie. Both boys wanted the pie, and neither one was willing to give in. Reid had an idea. "I know, Jerry, let me make you my super-duper-deluxe sundae with cottage cheese, bananas, and whipping cream. It will be much better than the pie!"

Jerry relinquished the pie to Reid.

"I want to be the mother," said Jill.

"No, I want to be the mother," said Jan.

"You be the baby," said Jill.

"No, You be the baby," said Jan.

STORY #1
PLAYING
HOUSE

Discussion Questions:

1. How could the girls solve this problem?
2. What is another way?
3. Can you think of three different ways of solving the problem?
4. What would you want to do?
5. What should the teacher (or the mother) do?

Additional suggestions using the same story format:

1. Both children want to be teacher.
2. Both children want to be Wonder Woman.
3. Both children want to be the Six-Million Dollar Man.
4. Both children want to be Daddy.
5. Both children want to wear the long white dress.
6. Both children want to wear the cowboy hat.
7. Both children want to use the truck.
8. Both children want to ride the trike.
9. Both children want to swing on the swing.
10. Both children want all the (blocks, clay dough, Legos, crackers, apples, doll clothes, puppets, finger paints).

117

11. Both children want to work on the typewriter.
12. Both children want to carry the juice to the table.
13. Both children want to serve the crackers.

It was lunch time, and the children were washing their hands. Jan and Ann were arguing about who was going to sit by the teacher, Mrs. Smith.

"It's my turn to sit by her today," said Jean.

"No, it is not," said Ann. "You sat by her last time. It's my turn."

"No, it isn't," said Jean.

"Yes, it is," said Ann.

The argument continued until Miss Gibbons asked the girls to stop arguing and come to lunch. She told them she remembered that Ann had sat by Mrs. Smith yesterday and so today it was Jean's turn.

"I don't care," said Ann. "Mrs. Smith is a dumb teacher, anyway."

"You shouldn't talk that way about Mrs. Smith," said Miss Gibbons. "Mrs. Smith would not like that."

"I don't care," said Ann. "I hate the whole school."

"Well, you stop talking like that and come to lunch now," said Miss Gibbons.

Ann hurried over to the table before any of the rest of the children and sat down on the end. Jean sat next to Ann and saved a place for Mrs. Smith.

"It's my turn to sit by you, Mrs. Smith," Jean shouted. "Come and sit here by me." Jean was very happy that she had won the argument with the help of Miss Gibbons. Ann was not happy. She was very angry.

Discussion Questions:

1. Why did Ann act the way she did?
2. Was it right for the girls to argue?
3. Was it good for the teacher (Miss Gibbons) to tell Jean that she could sit by Mrs. Smith?
4. How do you think Ann felt when Miss Gibbons told her that she shouldn't "talk that way" about Mrs. Smith?
5. Why do you think Ann took Jean's meat?
   a. Was she hungry?
   b. She just couldn't wait?
   c. She didn't have any breakfast?
   d. She wanted to get back at Jean?
   e. She didn't like to say the blessing?
6. What do you think the teacher should do now that Ann had taken the meat?
7. How would you feel if you were Ann?
8. How would you feel if you were Jean?

The children should be helped to see both sides of this story. They should "feel" something for both girls as well as both teachers. This situation presents problems

119

for everyone. They should also be helped to see that the solutions are not always easy. The children should be helped to find a better form of discipline for Ann's behavior than physical punishment. The logical consequence, of course, would be for Ann to give Jean her meat. The teacher should then point out that the teacher in this situation could talk about the emotions the girls are feeling (anger) and that it is okay to feel that way, but it is not good manners to take someone else's meat.

The children all got ready for the blessing and said, "God is great, God is good. Let us thank him for our food. Amen."

While the prayer was being said, Ann reached over and took Jean's piece of meat and stuffed it into her mouth.

When Jean opened her eyes and saw that her meat was gone and that Ann had stuffed it in her mouth, she began to complain.

"Ann took my meat, and now I have no meat," she said. "I am going to take hers."

11
TRUTH
AND
LYING

"I saw Jaws in the bathroom just now."

"That's not true. Jaws couldn't get in our bathroom. He's too big."

"I know, I was just teasing."

Children often do not speak the truth. Their imaginations are extremely creative. What seems to be a lie or an untruth to an adult may be to them simply a fun story. However, children often believe what they say, and because of their restricted understanding of reality, they believe a story that is obviously not true. Young children have difficulty understanding the difference between fantasy and reality and therefore are not always aware they are telling an untruth.

"I got a million dollars."

"You don't either; you only have seven dollars."

This young child's inability to understand numbers and amounts of money has led him to think that when he has what seems to be a lot of money, it must be about a million dollars.

"We live on a farm and have a dog and chickens and cows and pigs."

"You do? I didn't know you lived on a farm."

This young child may *wish* he lived on a farm, and perhaps he thinks by telling someone he does live on a farm, this wish might come true.

* * * * *

Before discussing the problem of lying, we must understand the child. Between the ages of four and six he tells tall tales; he has a difficult time understanding the difference between reality and fantasy; and he has gained tremendous "word power"

121

in the past two or three years and seems to love to hear himself tell stories. Also, many children like to impress other children and adults by telling make-believe stories. The child's imagination at this stage is vivid, and he or she is tremendously creative. Consider the following examples of tall tales told by a kindergarten child:

John was riding in the back of the car as Gary's mother drove the children home from the birthday party. It was snowing outside and was very cold. The winter had been cold and long this year. "Have you been having fun at your house this winter, John? What are some of the things you have been doing?" asked Gary's mother as she drove along the highway.

"Yes, we've been having fun at my house," said John. "We've been climbing trees, and we even found a bird's nest."

"You have been climbing trees and finding bird's nests in the winter?" said mother.

"Yeh," said John. "And you know what was in it (the nest)?"

"What?"

"Um, an egg. And it cracked open, and guess what came out? Well, it was a baby chicken."

"You saw a baby chicken come out of an egg that came from a nest up in the tree in the middle of the cold winter?"

"Yep." said John. "And we cooked the chicken and ate it for supper."

* * * * *

This child was having a wonderful time telling a story to his friend's mother. And the mother was having a wonderful time listening to him. She thought the stories he was telling were interesting and humorous.

What, then, is the difference between lying and "telling tall tales"? How can children be taught that truthfulness is a virtue they should acquire?

The difference between lying and telling "tall tales" seems to be in the *motives* of the child. If the child's motives are to *deceive* the adult, we could say the child is lying. The child who spills jam, then denies he did it is lying because he is attempting to deceive. The child who tells "tall tales" many times will know that the adult is playing along with him and knows the story is not true. Even if the adult does believe the story, the child will come back at some later date and tell the adult that he was "just teasing" or it was a made-up story.

One mother relates a discussion with her child's teacher during a parent conference. The mother asked the teacher if her

122

child told "tall tales." "Yes," said the teacher. "He is really cute when he tells them. He has such a vivid imagination. He told me once that a big black bear came into his back yard. Another time he told me that he lived on a farm, and another time he said that he was moving to Florida. Once he told me he had caught two stars out of the sky the night before. You know, though, he always comes back later in the day and tells me it was a made-up story, and I give him a big hug and say, 'I know.' "

Often children tell an untruth to an adult, but it is simply a *mismatch of what is real and what the child perceived.* The child who says "I saw an elephant bigger than this whole building" is simply expressing what he perceived to be true. Most adults accept this kind of exaggeration with a quiet "It must have been big, but probably not as big as this building."

Consider another reason why children tell untruths: often there is a *need to defend themselves.* Sometimes adults put children in an uncomfortable position from which the only way out seems to be to lie.

Adults using powerful rewards and punishments have expectations that must be met before the child can receive the reward and avoid the pain of punishment. The only way for the child to circumvent these pressures is to lie. When these children make mistakes, they must either miss out on a reward or receive a punishment. If they tell the truth, they will be punished. If they lie, they can avoid the punishment, or at least delay the punishment until the lie is detected. With such options, children will deceive in order to protect themselves. The common solution to this deception is to make the punishment for lying more severe than all other punishments. Unfortunately, this solution builds up a more intense and punitive environment. It is wiser to foster honesty than to suppress dishonesty.

How do parents and teachers teach children to value truthfulness?

• *Model Honesty.* Children are perceptive and learn that dishonesty is acceptable if the adult is dishonest. They learn from small acts, such as having a child tell someone on the phone the parents are not there, trying to get a teenager into the movie for a child's price, bringing pencils and paper home from the office, eating grapes that are not paid for at the grocery store, and not paying back a loan (even if it is a quarter) from a friend.

• *Call the child's attention to the real world.* When young children tell "tall tales," listen and enjoy the story; do not say anything punishing or humiliating. Remember, the child's creativity and imagination are at stake. Do let the child know, however, that you know it is a made up story. You could say something like, "What a fun and interesting story you told me. Boy, you can think of really good stories. It's fun to make up stories, isn't it?" Some children begin by telling tall tales and become very good at lying if they are not helped to realize the tall tales are not true.

Teachers and parents should limit a child's literature to stories that center around the child's world. A few fantasies mixed with the realistic can add variety, but too many can be confusing to a child. Many adults remember some of the stories told to them as youngsters and how confused they became about the truth of the story. Fantasies can be frightening to young children. Since many stories written for young children center around their realistic world, focusing on these kinds of stories will help the young child understand the difference between reality and fantasy.

• *Help a child see the exact match between what he says and what is real.* When he says that Jaws might come into the bathroom, help him understand that Jaws is too big to come into the bathroom. When the child says that the snake he saw was longer than the school bus, talk to him about how long the snake really was and perhaps make a clay-dough snake so that he can try to remember the approximate length.

• *Tolerate an inexact match between what a child says and what is real.* Adults sometimes try to be too literal. Saying something like "It *seemed* to be about that long to you, didn't it?" is effective.

• *Try not to put children into positions in which there is no way out but to lie or to lose self-esteem.* Some situations occur in which there is no reason to make an issue of a child's statement. Recognizing there are situations from which the only way out is to lie does not mean that lying is right; it means only that an adult should try to understand why it happens. A good example of this is the story of a child who was caught by his father playing "doctor" with the girls. The boy was so embarrassed that he wanted the entire episode to be forgotten. When his father asked him what had happened in there, he said that nothing had happened, that they were just playing. Pressing the issue would have been humiliating for the child. If, however, the incident should occur again or the father should see that the child is trying to deceive in other situations, he should take further action.

- *Summary*
- Try to *understand* why a child is trying to deceive. Are there problems in his life that need attention? Does he receive a great deal of attention and special treatment (reinforcement) when he tells lies?
- *Don't press or force some issues* that will frighten the child about an action that is less important than lying.
- *Teach* a child through example and techniques (stories, lessons, role playing) that "honesty is the best policy."
- *Expect and trust in honest* behavior from your child. Children usually live up to expectations. Sometimes a child will become honest because an adult trusts him.
- *Communicate.* Listen to your children. Be aware of what he is doing.
- *Avoid punishment* but use logical consequences when a child does not have to deceive an adult to avoid punishment. A direct relationship exists between an increase in punishment and an increase in deceptiveness.

Shane had just come home from school. Mother was so happy to see him. Shane and mother sat down at the table and had some cookies and milk. "Did you have a nice day at school, Shane?" Yes," Shane responded with a mouthful of cookies. "We got to play in the gym today; and we had ice cream for lunch. I told the teacher that we lived on a farm."

"But we don't live on a farm," said Mother. "That is not a true story."

"I know, said Shane laughingly, "but I just told her anyway, and I also told her that we went to Florida this summer; I mean last summer."

"But we didn't go to Florida," said mother. "We have never been to Florida."

"I know, said Shane. "But it was fun to tell her that anyway. She was real nice and said, 'You did?' "

Mother didn't know what to do. She didn't want her little boy, Shane, to grow up telling lies. She tried to think of the best way of handling the problem. She thought of these ideas. You tell which one you think might be the best idea:

· Spank him so he won't tell lies any more.
· Yell at him and tell him that he is a very naughty boy for telling all those lies.
· Make him go to his room without supper.
· Make him wash his mouth out with soap for telling lies.
· Change the subject
· Laugh at him and tell him that he tells funny

stories. Tell him that it is fun to make up stories and that boys and girls who are five and six years old become especially good at making up stories, but they should remember that they are stories and be sure to tell the teacher it was just a "made up" story. Don't say any more about it.

After a discussion on the various courses of actions to take, help a child see that the last action would be best—that the child needs to know it is best to tell the truth, but that it is also fun to make up stories. Most children at age five or six tell "tall tales." They should know that though it is fun to tell tall tales, it can become a habit and that the stories become ways of not telling the truth. If a child responds that some of the more severe punishment should be used, help him empathize with the child in the story by putting himself in that child's place. The teacher could ask, "What if that were you? What would you want your parents to do?"

Discussion Questions:

1. What did Greg do?
2. Why did he steal the candy?
3. Why did he lie to his mother about stealing the candy?
4. Was it all right for Greg to steal the candy since his mother wouldn't let him have any?
5. Why didn't his mother want him to have any candy?
6. What should mother do?
7. What should Greg do?
8. Do you think it would be best for mother to spank Greg or do you think it would be best for her to go to the store man and pay for the candy bar?

In discussing stealing small items with young children, help them to see that it is not only wrong because stealing is wrong but because it hurts another individual. Try to help them see that if they were the store man, they wouldn't want children taking candy bars from their store because they would lose money. One candy bar doesn't cost very much, but if everyone took a

Greg had just been to the store with his mother. As they were going through the check stand, Greg decided he would like some candy. He started to ask his mother to buy him some, but he knew she wouldn't because she had told him candy isn't good for little boys. Greg wanted the candy so much he decided to take it. He knew it was wrong, but he still wanted the candy. While mother wasn't looking, Greg took the candy and put it in his pocket.

Mother finished checking out her groceries and carried them to the car. Greg could hardly wait until he got into the car to eat his candy bar. While mother was driving, he ate it. It was so good, he was happy he had taken it. Mother would never have let him have it. When Greg

128

and mother arrived home, mother saw that Greg had some chocolate on his face.

"Where did you get the chocolate on your face, Greg?" Mother asked.

"I don't know; it must of just camed there." Greg said.

"Did you eat a candy bar or something?" Mother asked.

Greg was getting a little nervous and said, "No, mother. I guess that is left over from the last time I had a candy bar—last year or something."

"Greg, I want you to tell me the truth. Did you take a candy bar from the store and eat it?" asked mother.

"Yes," said Greg. But you wouldn't buy me one, and I really wanted it."

candy bar, it would cost the store man a lot.

Role Play:

Allow the children to role play the above story. Add a store man to the story, and have the children come in at the end and pay for the candy bar with his own money. Have the store man act very happy that the boy decided to pay for the candy, and have the store man tell him that he hopes he won't take things from stores again. Allow the children to play the different roles so that they can gain an understanding of each role from a first-hand perspective.

STORY #3
PRETENDING

Discussion Questions:

1. What did Karen and Marilyn tell Christine?
2. Did Karen and Marilyn tell the truth?
3. Why did they tell Christine those stories?
4. How did it make Christine feel?
5. How would you feel if you were Christine?
6. What should the girls do now?
7. Is it all right to tell stories that are not true?

Karen and Marilyn went to Grandma's house to stay for two weeks. They always loved to go to Grandma's house because there was so much to do on the farm—playing in the barns and on the hay stacks and with Grandma's organ. A little girl named Christine lived next door. Christine didn't have very much money and always looked dirty. She never combed her hair or washed her face.

Karen and Marilyn didn't have very much money either, but they liked to pretend they did. They told Christine about the big house they lived in that had 100 rooms. They told her they had diamond dresses and mink coats at home but didn't want to bring them to Grandma's house. They told her they had a lot of maids who did all the work so they didn't ever have to do any. They told her their daddy let them buy whatever they wanted, and they could get ice cream and candy anytime they wanted to.

Christine felt bad. She didn't have any money. Her clothes were ragged, and her house was old and worn out. She never had any money and could never buy anything she wanted. She wished she could be like Karen and Marilyn and have diamond dresses and all the ice cream she wanted.

Discussion Questions:

1. What happened?
2. What did the girls do wrong?
3. Why did they jump on the bed?
4. Was it okay to let their friends come in the house while their mother was gone?
5. Was the bed-breaking their friends' fault?
6. Why did the girls tell their mother that the bed broke by itself?
7. Was that a lie?
8. What should the mother do?
9. What should the girls do?
10. How did the girls feel?
11. How did the mother feel?
12. How would you feel if you were the girls?
13. What would you do?

Help the children discover the most fair way to deal with the problem of lying. Help them discover a logical consequence that would be fair and something the girls would learn from rather than a harsh punishment. Young children typically resort to spanking as the best

Mother had to go to the grocery store. "You girls stay here and be good while I am at the grocery store. I will be back in about an hour; so be sure and stay in the house." Trisha and Kari played quietly with their dolls for awhile. The door bell rang. It was their very best friends. "Can you come out and play?" their friends asked.

"No, we have to stay in the house until mother gets back," said Trisha.

"Then can we come in and play with you?" their friends said.

"Well, we aren't supposed to have friends in the house while mother is gone, but I guess it won't hurt for a little while," said Trisha.

So the four girls played together with the dolls until they became tired of playing dolls. "Let's jump on the bed," said Kari.

"Okay," said Trisha, "but be careful so you won't break it." The four girls jumped and jumped and jumped. They were having so much fun when suddenly—kerplop—the bed broke.

"Oh, no," said Trisha. "Mother will be really mad. You better go home before mother gets here," she said to her friends.

After their friends left, mother returned. The girls quickly came out of the bedroom and closed the door.

"How did everything go?" asked Mother.

"All right," said the girls.

"Did you have any problems?"

"No," said the girls.

Mother walked in the bedroom to put away some new socks she had bought the girls. "Oh, my goodness, what happened to the bed?" asked mother.

"It just fell down by itself," said Kari. "We didn't do anything."

punishment because they know of nothing else, even though they don't want to be spanked themselves.

12 RESPECT FOR PROPERTY VERSUS DESTRUC- TIVENESS

A teacher finds that while she was out of the room Joshua tore the pages out of the story book.

A mother finds the walls covered with crayon drawings.

A teacher finds the new plastic truck shattered by blows from a hammer.

A child pokes holes in the sliding screen door with a pencil.

Such waste and destructiveness prompt the adult to ask in astonishment, "Why?"

Usually these acts of property destruction occur when the adult is out of the room, but respect for property should exist when the child is alone. Not only children, however, but adults also show more respect for property when others are around. For example, throwing gum wrappers on the floor, cutting across the grass instead of walking on the sidewalk, and throwing trash out the window of the car are examples of acts adults usually do not perform in the presence of others—only when others are not around. Young children are not as socialized as adults, and usually do not care whether someone else is watching. Adults cringe at some of the antics of young children involving the use of personal property, such as swinging on doors, climbing on cabinets, walking on furniture, scratching chairs with a fork, writing on walls, and many other such acts of destruction.

How can we as adults teach children respect for property? Consider first some of the possible reasons for children's showing disrespect:

● *Ignorance of value.* Very young children possesses neither the cognitive and physical ability nor the experience to know what

135

is valuable and what is not until parents teach them. A child between the ages of one and three is interacting with his environment in a sensory-motor way. He grows, develops, and learns by touching, smelling, tasting, seeing, and hearing. He handles objects in the ways that are familiar to him: banging, throwing, pushing, pulling, tasting, patting, stomping, and biting. This young child does not understand that Mommy's books are valuable and should not be thrown on the floor. Through many experiences of having Mother pick up her books and say, "No, Mommy's books," and take the child over to his books and say, "You can play with your books," the child might learn that he must show respect for Mommy's books but need not act the same way toward his own.

As children grow older, they gradually acquire the ability to respect other people's property through experiences such as the one above, in which mother set the limits. Note that the child is allowed to be destructive with his property but not with another person's, even if the items are the same.

Some children, however, are not taught the value of property. They are allowed to roam anywhere in the classroom or the house and to treat objects as they desire. As a consequence, when they are taken with their parents to visit friends, they roam through the friend's house, get into drawers, knock over things, and put on lipstick they find in a bathroom. No one likes this child to visit because they know the house will become a wreck before they leave.

• *Rebellion.* Now the opposite: some adults are so strict with what a child can touch and not touch, what he can and cannot mess up, where he can and cannot play with things, where he can and cannot bring his friends, that the child often rebels and becomes destructive in other environments, such as at school or in other people's homes. One mother who kept an absolutely spotless house made family members and others remove their shoes when they entered, made her six-year-old son strip in the yard so he wouldn't mess up the house with his dirty clothes. Several children in this family later rebelled. One day one of the girls wrote all over her bedroom walls with lipstick, an act she knew would hurt and anger her mother.

• *Curiosity.* Sometimes young children do not intend to damage property; they are curious and need to explore. Because of their inept manipulative skills, often they are clumsy and break or tear things. The holes made in a screen door or the dismantled clock or toy sometimes fall into this category. The need to manipulate tools is strong in a young child and no doubt is be-

136

hind the expression, "Give a child a hammer and you will find that everything needs hammering."

● *Environment not organized to meet the needs of the child.* When a young couple with their new baby went out to buy their first set of living room furniture, the salesman asked them, "Are you *furniture-oriented* or *child-oriented*?" The couple quickly responded, "We are child-centered."

"Then let me suggest this beautiful Naugahide couch and chair set. It will give you years of wear with your little ones and will look nice in your living room as well," said the salesman.

Too often parents do not organize the environment to meet the needs of the child. Precious figurines are left on a shelf within reach of the baby; hammers and sharp objects are left on a shelf; and of course these not only hurt furniture, they also hurt the child. Obviously, young children do not have very much sense about the use of tools and the protection of valuable things. A child observes his dad hammering a nail in the table down in the basement; so within a few minutes he hammers a nail in the coffee table up in the living room.

The preschool environment should be organized so that children can have successful and safe experiences. Damage to property is often not intended but is the fault of the organization of space and materials. If a child has to carry water from the housekeeping area, across the room, through the book-keeping corner, and past the block corner, you may count on something becoming wet. Materials and equipment should be stored in the area where they will be used. Those items to be used by children should be easily accessible to them, and those items not to be used by them should be inaccessible.

● *Venting feelings.* "In our house we slammed doors when we got angry until we broke all the doors and Dad wouldn't let us slam them anymore."

"In our house mother threw dishes when she got angry."

Many of us have had the experience of either damaging property or seeing someone else damage it while venting feelings. This is irresponsible behavior, and unfortunately adults model this behavior for children.

In young children's behavior a destructive response is quite frequent. For example, a child doesn't like the picture he drew, so he tears up his picture and also his friends' pictures. A child can't get the blocks to stack without falling, so he throws the blocks and breaks a window. A child has been put on a chair in the "time-out" section of the room for misbehavior and knocks all the teacher's books onto the floor. A child comes into nursery school after just having had a spanking by his mother and knocks over the easel paint.

That many young children engage in this type of behavior, however, does not make it right. It is not something adults must tolerate. Steps should be taken to help the child find alternative ways to vent his feelings. At one time, researchers in the area of aggressive behavior in young children advocated having children "beat the Bozo clown" or something of that nature. This is known as the "catharsis hypothesis." Other people in the field, however, feel that this type of behavior produces more destructiveness than less and encourages and reinforces the child's aggressive behavior.

The better solution for destructive behavior is to redirect the child's behavior into something productive and fulfilling. Beating on Bozo does not seem to fulfill these goals for most children. Making a car with the woodworking tool, however, might help the child vent his feelings productively and would be fulfilling. Other effective activities might be making bread, baking cookies, working with clay dough, playing rhythm instruments, dancing or moving to instrument, and tumbling on a tumbling mat. These activities might help the child vent feelings at the same time.

● *Reinforcement.* Adults often unwittingly reinforce a child's destructive behavior through both negative and positive means. One mother tells of a friend who frequently visited her. While she was talking to the friend, the friend's little boy raided the drawers in the bedroom, spilled perfume, and squeezed toothpaste in the bathroom. when the child's mother finally went to check on him and saw what he had done, she picked him up and gave him a hug and said, "Now, now! We mustn't get into other people's things. Okay?"

The child smiled and said, "Okay." But the next time they visited, he did the same thing again. The woman was both permissive and reinforcing of the child's behavior.

Parents and teachers often reinforce a child's destructive behavior by punishing it. Some children are destructive for the attention they get in the form of punishment. Negative attention, for these children, is better than no attention at all. While a parent is talking on the phone, for example, a child will engage in destructive behavior to capture his or her attention. An account from one mother about her child's scraping the ashes from the fireplace onto the floor and vacuuming water out of the toilet are examples of a child who desires attention from a mother talking on the phone.

138

• *Change in environment.* Children are sensitive to a change in environment even though that change may seem slight to a parent or a teacher. A new baby in the family; moving to a new home (even if it is just down the street); marital conflict between Mom and Dad; the homecoming of a parent after an extended period of time; the moving away of a friend; stress in a parent's life, such as a new job or problems at work; new friends; physical illness; change of schools; relatives coming to stay or live with the family, and so on, are changes likely to precipitate some destructive behavior.

Though these changes in the child's environment do not make the destructive behavior acceptable, being aware of their effect helps the adult understand why the child is behaving as he is.

• *Modeling.* As adults, we expect behavior from a child that we are not necessarily willing to exhibit ourselves. For example, one parent tells the story of Niko, his son, who was tearing the screen on the door with his ski poles.

"I don't want you to do that again, Son, or I'll have to put your ski poles up," said Dad.

Dad had the screen fixed, and in a few weeks the same thing happened again. Dad was so angry this time that instead of following through with what he had said about putting the ski poles up, he grabbed the ski poles and broke them in the hall across his knee. The other children in the family stood and stared.

The father had told his children, by his behavior, that when you are really angry and someone has done something wrong, it is all right to be destructive. As we mentioned earlier, other examples of parents' destructive behavior, such as breaking dishes, slamming doors, and throwing breakable items model for children the very behavior adults do not approve of in them. It must seem strange to children, especially after having been lectured about being careful with the walls and the furniture, to see an adult hammering nails into the wall.

• *Lack of respect and feelings of empathy for other people and their property.* As we discussed in the section on empathy, young children need experience, modeling, and teaching from an adult to be empathetic toward others. Some children never seem to learn this and grow up without sufficient feeling for those around them and for their property. To change this behavior, parents and teachers again need to focus on the needs and feelings of others and help the child become responsive to them. Destructive behavior should accordingly diminish without special attention.

Now that we have examined the possible reasons for a child's engaging in destructive behavior, let us look at what parents and teachers can do to help the child change this behavior.

• *Teach children to respect and value their own property and the property of others.* One parent uses the saying "Let's not *break* our house" or "Let's not *hurt* our house." Helping children to be proud of what they have and to take care of it can help them respect the property of others. It is a good idea when children are young to "child proof" the house and put away valuable items. Some parents reject this idea, saying that children will not learn to be careful and that when they go to someone else's house they will "get into everything." This does not seem to be the case. Young children have a difficult time remembering from one time to the next and usually do not strongly generalize from the home situation to the neighbor's house. Setting limits and teaching children they are not to "get into things" in other people's houses is a more direct and efficient approach. Both verbal and physical guidance must be used in enforcing these limits by telling the child what you expect and then following through, leading the child by the hand or picking him up if necessary.

A parent might say, "When we go to Mrs. Smith's house, you stay with me and don't wander around the house. Mrs. Smith has a lot of little things that are special to her, and she does not want anyone playing with them." While visiting at the Smith home, if the child starts to "get into things," Mother needs to follow through with what she told the child and quietly lift him into her arms, saying, "You'll have to sit with mother on the couch. Remember, I asked you not to get into the things at Mrs. Smith's house, and you did so. You stay here with me." The preschool teacher must educate the children in advance about what is acceptable behavior when a child is visiting new places.

• *Understand the child.* When a child is observed participating in destructive behavior, the adult needs to look at the situation and try to understand why the child is behaving so. Considering any of the reasons suggested earlier in this chapter might be helpful in understanding the behavior of the child.

• *Help the child learn positive and constructive ways of expressing feelings.* A child often acts destructively because of feelings of hostility, anger, rebellion, sadness, depression, frustration, humiliation, guilt, insecurity, need for attention, and others. The child can try to understand how the child feels, then help him redirect his behavior into positive channels—behavior constructive and self-fulfilling.

140

• *Allow the child freedom within limits.* As we discussed under the section on rebellion, if a child's environment is severely limited, he may rebel and become destructive. If, on the other hand, a child is given complete freedom and is not taught to respect the property of others, he will also be destructive. Children should be allowed to explore their environment because they are innately curious, but this should not be done at the expense of others' property. Limits must be set in order for the child to learn respect for others.

A good example of how a parent or teacher can allow a child freedom within limits is to give the child who wants to paint a bucket of water and a paint brush. Most children will paint for hours. The child gets the same satisfaction painting with water as with paint. He can paint the sidewalks, the bricks or wood on the house or the school, the big rocks, poles, and fences, or whatever. Painting with water can even be done in the house or in the school with some supervision.

• *Structure and organize the environment to meet the needs of the child.* The environment in the home and the school should be organized and structured so that a young child can succeed and feel comfortable. The chance, then, of his being destructive is lessened.

• *Try to not reinforce destructive behavior.* If the child's destructive behavior has become a pattern, look at what is maintaining it. Why does the child continue to act in destructive ways? Is he being reinforced? Does he receive increased attention from you or others? Stop reinforcing his behavior.

• *Model behavior you would like the child to exhibit.* If you don't want the child to be destructive, don't be destructive yourself. If you want the child to value and respect property, do so yourself. An adult can show even a young toddler that he values and respects property. For example, a toddler may tear a page in a book. Instead of getting angry at the child or throwing the book away, the adult should get the scotch tape out and mend the book, showing the child that property is worth taking care of. The adult might say something like "Poor book. Look, it's all torn. We want to keep our books nice and pretty. Let's get some tape and tape it up. Here, you help me. Now, doesn't that look better? The book is as good as new. We need to take very good care of our books because they are special to us."

• *Help the child empathize with others*—especially where there has been a loss of property or when property has been destroyed: "Poor little Richard's truck is broken. Now he doesn't have anything to play with. He must be very sad. Would you be sad if that happened to you?"

141

"I'm so sorry the Jones's kitchen caught on fire. They must feel terrible. What an awful thing to happen to such a fine family. We need to think of some ways that we can help them."

Help children verbalize feelings when they view destruction on television or in real life.

Dexter woke up early. Everyone else in the family was sound asleep. But since Dexter wasn't sleepy anymore and he couldn't go back to sleep, he decided to get up and play. First he played with his cars, but it wasn't any fun without someone else. Next, he decided to turn on the T.V. When he sat down on the couch, he noticed his mother's scissors there. Then Dexter got an idea.

Discussion Questions:
1. What happened?
2. What did Dexter do wrong?
3. Did Dexter mean to do a wrong thing?
4. Why did he make cuts in the couch?
5. What should his parents do?
6. What should Dexter do?
7. How does Dexter feel?
8. How do his parents feel?
9. How would you feel?
10. Have you ever done anything like that? Were you sorry?

He decided to cut up the couch just a little with the scissors. First he stuck the end of the scissors into the couch. It made funny little holes. Then he decided to make a few little cuts. Mother probably would never notice. Dexter made a few little cuts; then his hand slipped, and one of the little cuts turned into a great big cut. Now Dexter got scared, and he hurried back to bed.

About a half an hour later Mother got up for the day, and as usual she walked into the living room. When she saw the couch she yelled, "Henry, come and see what someone has done to the couch!" The noise was so loud that the other children got up and ran into the living room.

Four children were dressed in pajamas in the living room. Father asked angrily, "Now which one of you children did this?" The children all shook their heads and said, "Not me." Even Dexter said, "Not me."

"Maybe a burglar did it during the night," said Dexter.

"I don't think so," said Dad. "The person is right in this family."

The children at the nursery school were participating in book time. Each child sat on the rug, looking at whatever book they wanted. Then the teacher said, "It's time to put up the books so we can go see the fire engine." The children became so excited to see the fire engine that many of them left their books on the floor. Several of the children even stepped on the books as they ran to get their coats on.

The teacher saw the books all over the floor and said, "Children, we cannot see the fire engine until all the books are picked up." The children ran over to pick up the books, but they were still excited and were not careful. They quickly picked up the books, and instead of placing them nicely on the shelf, they threw and pushed them onto the shelf. One little boy even tore the cover off one book.

Now the teacher became even more angry.

Discussion Questions:
1. What happened?
2. What did the children do that was wrong?
3. Did the children mean to do the wrong thing?
4. Why did the children treat the books as they did?
5. What should the teacher do?
6. What should the children do?
7. How did the teacher feel?
8. How did the children feel?
9. What should the teacher do to help the children learn to take care of their books?

13
UNDER-STANDING RULES VERSUS ANTI-SOCIAL CONDUCT

Rules are important. Without them our world would be confusing. Young children are dependent upon rules to help guide their behavior. Rules provide order and regularity to a child's world and make his environment predictable. However, understanding rules is not so simple, even for adults.

Most parents and teachers would say they like their children to "obey rules." If asked specifically whether it would be important for children to "understand" rules, some adults would say, "Yes, it is important," and other adults would say, "Not really. The most important thing is that children *obey* rules." If the latter adults were asked what their *long-range* goals are for their children, they would all probably say, "to be healthy, happy, well-adjusted, self-directed, able to make decisions, and to think for themselves." To achieve these long-range goals, young children not only must learn to obey rules but also gain an understanding of them.

Piaget (1932) noted that young children confuse the more abstract moral and social rules with the permanent and regular physical laws of the universe. Because of young children's deep respect and deference to adult authority, they tend to consider rules described by adults as fixed and unalterable. Talking with a seven-year-old boy about playing marbles on a field that is triangular rather than the usual square, Piaget asked:

"Is it as fair a game as the [other game] you showed me?"

"No."

"Why?"

"Because it isn't a square."

"And if everyone played that way, even the big children, would it be fair?"

"No."

"Why not?"

"Because it isn't a square."

The rigidity of this child toward adapting the rules of the game will be altered when he confronts similar problems in the course of growing up. He will find that rules for games and social conventions are usually based on cooperation rather than on universal laws. Increased social interaction will help the child become more flexible.

Unfortunately, the needed social learning situations are not readily available or regular in occurrence; thus many children remain unnecessarily rigid in their understanding of rules.

TYPES OF RULES   For children and adults there are two types of rules. One is *explicit* rules and the other is *implicit* rules. An *explicit* rule is a rule that is very specific. It is all spelled out and tells the child exactly what he is supposed to do. An example of an explicit rule is: "At 10 a.m. all the coats must be hung up in the lockers."

An *implicit* rule is more broad. It is a guide to behavior rather than a specific rule. Here is an example of an implicit rule: "We must take care of our clothes." This rule has a higher expectation than "hanging up coats."

In helping children become morally mature, the adult should try to move from explicit rules to implicit rules for the following reasons:
- To help children think for themselves.
- To help them see that most rules are changeable and man-made.

As an example, the New Testament portrays Jesus's implicit rules rather than explicit rules. In Palestine there were many explicit rules, but Jesus proposed that it was the "spirit" of the law that needed to be lived; he gave implicit rules, such as, "Love thy neighbor" rather than "Every Tuesday, take a cake over to the neighbor across the street." "Love thy neighbor" implies a much higher expectation than the explicit rule stated above.
- To help children see that rules are not necessarily restrictions and not always absolutes but are guides or conventions to help us interact and enjoy life better.
- To help children become responsible for their behavior.
- To allow children to make up their own "explicit rules" that will help them live the "implicit rules." For example, a teacher might say, "We would like to have a nice, quiet, orderly class-

148

room. Let us think of some rules that will help us have a quiet, orderly classroom." The children might suggest the following rules:
- Be quiet when the teacher is talking.
- Help clean up after snacking.
- Help clean up after finger painting.
- Help clean up after free play.
- Don't all talk at the same time. Take turns.
- Put all your things in your locker.
- Be quiet at nap time.
- Help the teacher when she wants you to help.
- When it's time to go home, put up your things.

If children are allowed to make up their own rules, they will be more likely to follow them. Teachers and parents need to be careful, however, that not too many rules are set up because the young child will be overwhelmed and will not be able to remember or comply with all of them

Young children live with a combination of explicit rules and implicit rules. The desirable direction should be to move toward the use of implicit rules, but the use of some explicit rules at a young age is both important and necessary. Young children feel secure when there are rules. They often make up rules if they feel that the environment is unfair. For example, after Ken ran away and hid when it was his turn to do the dishes, Larry said to mother, "We should have a rule around here that if anyone runs away when it is their turn to do the dishes, they should have to do them every night for the next week." Children tend to be very punitive toward another child when it comes to deciding what the consequences should be for one who doesn't obey the rules.

Why do some children *not* obey rules and engage in antisocial behavior? Some possible explanations would include the following:
- To show parents and teachers "who's the boss."
- To gain attention.
- To hurt others.
- To express feelings of despair: "I don't care."
- Permissive parents: not taught in the home to obey rules.
- Authoritarian parents: too much stress upon strict obedience of rules.
- Too much focus on explicit rules rather than implicit rules.
- Lack of understanding of rules.
- Too many rules.
- Environment not supportive of the rules that need to be followed.

- Venting feelings.
- Modeling: adults do not obey rules. A good example of this is when a child is told not to eat anything before dinner, then sees his parent eating.

To help a child follow rules and engage in less antisocial behavior, follow the suggestions in the previous chapter on respect for property, and don't forget to focus more on implicit rules than on explicit rules.

Another suggestion to help children understand rules is to *discuss* the rule with the child so that he clearly understands it and the consequences for not following it. It is an unwise adult who establishes a rule, then does not explain it to the child. Children, like adults, often push until they are told to stop. Children need to know exactly where their limitations are.

Another important suggestion to help children understand rules is to respect them and be willing to listen to their comments on the value and the implementation of the rule. Consider the following true example:

The kindergarten children loved to play with the blocks. Every day during the first hour, the teacher let the children take the blocks out and play with them. After free play was over, it was time to get into groups for learning time. Every day, the same thing happened: the children did not want to put away the blocks.

"Well, I didn't get them out," said one child.

"I didn't get them out, either," said another child.

"Jan and Jay played with them last," said one child.

"Mike got them out first," said Jan and Jay.

This conversation went on every day until one day the teacher said, "Well, I'm sorry, but we will not be able to play with the blocks any more this year because no one will be responsible for picking up the blocks."

Several days went by, and the children were not allowed to play with the blocks. The children were sad. They wanted to build bridges and forts, but the teacher had said, "No block playing for the rest of the year."

Shane thought and thought about this problem. He thought about how he always picked up the blocks when he played with them and that it didn't seem fair that all the children should be punished. So he went up to the teacher and said, "Miss Sterrett, it's not fair that all of us can't play with the blocks."

"Well, Shane," said Miss Sterrett, "I'm sorry, but some of the children will not pick up the blocks, so I decided that no one can play with them."

Shane thought and thought about this and then asked, "Well, what good does it do to have blocks when you can't even play with them?"

Miss Sterrett laughed and said, "You're right, Shane, it is a pretty silly rule. Let's talk to the class and see if we can think of some way that everyone can play with the blocks and also help pick them up."

The teacher discussed the problem with the children, and they decided that everyone in the class, whether they played with the blocks or not, would help clean them up. They would try this for awhile to see if it worked. If it didn't, they would try something else. It was important, however, that every class feel responsible for cleaning up the room before group-learning time. Because of Shane and because the teacher respected a young child's opinion and ideas, the children in the classroom were able to play with the blocks again.

STORY #1
PLAYING AT
NAP TIME

Discussion Questions:

1. What happened in the story?
2. Why didn't Kim want to take a nap?
3. What should the teacher do?
4. What should Kim do?
5. How does the teacher feel?
6. How does Kim feel?
7. How would you feel?
8. What would you do?

At Kim's nursery school there are lots of rules, but there is one rule that Kim doesn't like. The rule is that everyone has to lie down and be quiet during nap time. Kim doesn't even like to sleep. She only likes to play. Kim hates to lie down on her cot when it would be much more fun to play in the housekeeping area with the blocks and puzzles, or even play outside.

Kim always asked if she could do something else besides take a nap, and then she would get angry at the teachers because they always told her "no." One day at nap time, Kim decided she was *not* going to take a nap. So she got up from her cot and went over to the housekeeping area and started to play house.

The teacher quietly walked over to Kim and said, "Kim, lie down on your cot now. It is nap time. You can play in the housekeeping area after nap."

"I don't want to take a nap," screamed Kim. "I want to play house. You can't make me take a nap."

The teacher insisted. "I'm sorry, Kim. It is nap time. Do you want to walk or be carried back to your cot?"

Kim started to kick and scream. "I'm not going. You can't make me. I want to play house."

Discussion Questions:

1. What happened in the story?
2. What did Allen do wrong?
3. Did Allen know the rule about having good manners at the table?
4. Did mother and Dad do the right thing?
5. How did Allen feel?
6. Was it fair that Allen be charged a dollar for burping?
7. How would you feel if you were Allen?
8. How did Allen's parents feel?
9. Do you think Allen will keep burping at the table?

At the Johnson home there is a rule that everyone will use good manners at the table. Every night Allen burps at the table. Mother gets angry and sends him to the bathroom. Father gets angry and tells Allen that he doesn't want to hear burping again at the table. The other children laugh because they think the burping is funny.

"Allen, what are we going to do about your burping?" Mother asked.

"I don't know," said Allen with a smile on his face. "I just can't help it."

154

"You can help it," said Father. "You have better control than that. I think since you can't seem to remember, we will charge you a dollar every time you burp at the table. Then the family can go out to dinner when we get enough money from your burping."

"That's not fair," said Allen. "I can't help it. I really can't."

"Well, that will be your problem," said father. "From now on *anyone* who burps at the table will have to pay a dollar to our dinner fund."

The rest of the children thought that was a great idea.

14
SELF-
CONTROL
VERSUS
GRATIFICA-
TION

This chapter will deal with the following behaviors:
- Self-control
- Delaying gratification
- Resistance to temptation
- Impulsiveness

If a young child does not have self-control, all other areas of moral development such as honesty, sharing, cooperation, kindness, respect for property, understanding others, and following rules are impaired. All of these areas involve a certain amount of self-control and self-discipline. For example, a child who has no self-control will not be honest if he has agreed not to eat anything before dinner and he is confronted with an opportunity to snitch a cupcake. A child without self-control will not be able to share his apple if he is hungry. He may consider the other child's needs, but in order to share, he must have self-control. A child without self-control will not cooperate because he wants everything for himself. A child without self-control will not respect property when his impulse is to destroy it. He will not comply with rules when they deter his immediate needs or desires.

Very few children have either a total lack of self-control or are totally self-controlled. Each child possesses a degree of self-control, some more than others.

The goals for parents and teachers is to help the child progress and gain a greater level of self-control, resistance to temptation, and the ability to delay gratification.

To delay immediate gratification in order to obtain a later and larger reward is an everyday experience for most people. Psychologists often point out that the ability to delay and postpone the satisfaction of immediate impulses is one mark of a mature person. The ability to delay a gratification is often called self-control, impulse control, or even a strong conscience.

Young children have a difficult time delaying gratification because they have not had enough experience to know that the promised gratification will actually come about. In fact, young children often do not understand exactly what "tomorrow" or "next week" mean.

Research can measure a child's ability to delay gratification by giving him a choice between a less valued object to be delivered now and a more valued object to be received at a later time. The child is asked to choose between the two.

In one test, the following sample questions were asked: "If your father offers you a choice between some money you can have right now or twice as much money in two months' time, which will you take?" Or, "A small notebook now or a larger notebook a week later; a small magnifying glass now or a larger one in a week; fifteen cents now or fifty cents in three weeks?" The children are told, "Be sure to choose what you would really take, because in one of the choices I will give you the thing you pick, although I won't tell you which until the end." The promise was always kept.

Temptations in the natural world usually offer immediately available gratification for the person if he yields. In order to resist, a child must learn to visualize or look forward to a long-term reward that may come later.

In other experiments, wherein children had to wait for the delayed for valued reward, they were more able to delay gratification if they engaged in thinking about something enjoyable. Even when rewards were not present during the delay period, the "think fun" group still had the longest periods of delay. Thinking about absent rewards made it difficult for children to delay gratification, as difficult as when the rewards were in front of them.

Clearly, if children are to be taught to delay gratification for long periods of time, it is better to assist them to think about enjoyable things rather than allow them to indulge in negative emotional states or to think about rewards yet to come.

The following true story is an example of a teacher who provided the children with a resistance-to-temptation practice, carefully supervised the activity, and reinforced the children's attempts at resisting temptation. The story will illustrate a learning situation that was developed when a natural experience was unavailable.

It was a beautiful day in Autumn, and the teacher had a lesson to teach the children about resistance to temptation. "This is such an important lesson for the children to learn," thought the teacher, "something they will use their entire life. How can I make it important to them?"

An idea came, and the teacher baked some cookies before the class began. She went into the classroom before the children arrived and placed a cookie on each chair. When the children arrived, the teacher purposely stayed out of the classroom for a few minutes. "Look," said the children, "cookies for us." Some of the children ate the cookies, and some of the children held theirs, waiting for the teacher to come in.

When the teacher came in she had some papers in one hand and some candy in the other. She looked around at the children and saw who had eaten the cookies and who had not. She said nothing to the children who *had* eaten their cookies but to those who did not she enthusiastically said to each one. "Good. I like the way you resisted temptation. You saved your cookie until you knew whether you could eat it or not. You are growing up because you can resist temptation." She then placed a sign on each of these children that said, "*I can resist temptation*" and gave them a piece of candy. Some of the other children who had eaten their cookies rebelled and complained that they did not get any candy. The teacher simply said, "The candy today is for those who resisted temptation. Maybe you could try another day."

The lesson that day consisted of talking to the children about the value of resisting temptation and having them tell of experiences in which they resisted temptation in their life. The focus was on the positive rather than the negative. An assignment was given to try at least one time to resist temptation at home that week, and they were told that next week they could report the experience to the class.

The next week came, and the teacher again used her "resistance to temptation" practice, but this time she put ice cream bars on the chairs. The children had the choice of letting the ice cream bars melt or receiving reinforcement for resisting the temptation to eat them.

Also on the table in the room was a large jar of candy. The teacher stayed out of the classroom for a few moments, then came in. None of the children had eaten any of the ice cream. None of the children had taken any of the candy. Again, the teacher verbally reinforced each one of the children by telling them how proud she was of them for resisting temptation. Again she put a sign around each child's neck that said, "*I can resist temptation,*" but this time she did one thing different. She gave each child a hug and told each how proud she was of him or her. She then gave each child two candies from the candy jar, and the children quietly said, "Thank you." The rest of the lesson that day consisted of the children's telling the teacher and the rest of the class about their experiences with resistance to temptation during the week. Each child reported at least one experience. The teacher supported and reinforced their attempts at resistance to temptation and helped the children understand how important resisting temptation is in their lives and how good they feel when they are able to control themselves. Some of the examples the children's experiences included the following:

"I was going to take a cookie before dinner; then I remembered to resist temptation, so I didn't take one."

"I wanted to beat up my brother because he broke my airplane; then I decided to resist temptation. So I didn't beat him up. I told him that he better not do it again."

"I wanted to eat my brother's cake before he came home from the baseball game. He would have never known the difference. But I decided to resist temptation and didn't eat it."

"I saw the baseball in the park that didn't look as if it belonged to anybody. I wanted to take it, but I decided to resist temptation. So I just left is sitting there, in case somebody came back looking for it."

Although contrived, this true classroom experience undoubtedly taught these young children to understand and resist temptation better than they had before.

It was Kathryn's birthday, and the children in the nursery school were busy making birthday cards for her. It was a special day for Kathryn. She could hardly wait until her mother brought the cupcakes for the class. While Kathryn was washing her hands after painting, her mother came in.

"Here are the cupcakes for Kathryn's party," said her mother. The cupcakes were beautiful. They were all decorated with white frosting and little colored candies. "Yum," said Kathryn. "Can we have one now, teacher?"

"No," said the teacher. "We are going to have them after lunch when we have your party. I will put them here on the cabinet until the party."

"Oh," said Kathryn. "Can I just look at them for a minute?"

"Yes," said the teacher. "That would be all right."

Kathryn looked at her beautiful cupcakes. They looked so good. She decided to count them just for fun. She counted 1 - 2 - 3 - 4 - 5 - 6 - 7 - 8 - 9 - 10 - 11 - 12 - 13 - 14 - 15 - 16 - 17 - 18 - 19 - and 20. Twenty cupcakes. Then Kathryn counted around the room. She counted all the children and the teacher. She counted only 19. There was one cupcake extra. Kathryn thought, "'Maybe I could sneak just one cupcake, and no one would know. There will still be enough for everyone in the class." Kathryn could not decide what to do.

STORY # 1
THE
BIRTHDAY
CUPCAKES

Discussion Questions:
1. What do you think Kathryn should do?
2. What would be the right thing to do?
3. Should she resist temptation?
4. What would happen if she made a mistake in counting?
5. What would you do?
6. What would the teacher do if she took a cupcake?
7. How would the teacher feel?

STORY #2
EATING
POPSICLES

Discussion Questions:

1. What happened in the story?
2. Did Bill make a right choice?
3. What would you have done?
4. Should his brothers and sisters have shared with him?
5. How do you think Bill felt?
6. How would you feel?
7. Is it better to wait for things, or is it better to have right now?

Mother bought some popsicles at the store. There were enough for each of the children in the family to have two. Mother suggested that the children eat one popsicle now and save the other for the next day when it would be hot.

"I want both of mine right now," said Bill.

"Wouldn't you rather wait until tomorrow when it will be hot outside?" said mother.

"I want both of mine now," said Bill.

The other children decided to eat one popsicle now and the other one the next day. They said to Bill, "You'll be sorry tomorrow when we have a popsicle and you won't."

Bill responded with, "No, I won't," as he ate his second popsicle.

The next day came. It was very hot. The children came into the house and got their popsicles out of the refrigerator. "Boy, do these taste good," they said.

Bill just watched. He didn't have any popsicle to eat. "You guys are just selfish. I don't have any popsicle, and you won't even share."

"You ate yours yesterday instead of waiting for today," said his brothers and sisters. "That was your choice."

162

What influences a child's development of self-control, delay of gratification, and resistance to temptation? Why do some children have high levels of self-control and others low levels? Possible reasons are as follows:

- *Inconsistency in disciplinary techniques.* At one time a child is punished for a certain behavior and at other times rewarded for the same behavior. At still other times the child is ignored for the same behavior. He cannot *predict* what his environment will be like and is less certain about the future.

- *Parents do not keep the promises* they make to the child. Some parents tend to threaten with punishment or try to bribe the child with rewards in order to control his behavior. When a parent promises a child candy tomorrow if he will give his brother's toy back today, he does not know whether he can *trust* what the parent says. Because of the child's past experience, he has learned that the parent's word cannot be trusted.

- *The child is either indulged or neglected or both.* In either case the child does not learn to resist temptation or delay gratification because he has not experienced the choices and delays needed to learn about future payoffs.

- *Parents model impulsiveness or lack of resistance to temptation.* The words a parent or a teacher says do not seem as important as the way they act. If a parent tells a child he should not steal, but the child sees the adult steal in one form or another, the child feels he can steal because the parent does.

- *Parents use extreme forms of power or punishment,* causing feelings of hostility and resentment in children. The child will learn, then, to avoid punishment but may even more strongly desire to do what is forbidden. To better understand this concept, read the following discussion on power ploys.

Power. Power techniques may be grouped into two basic approaches, one positive (reward) and the other negative (coercion). Both depend on external factors for their influence, and both are useful in obtaining obedience.

In spite of the similarities between reward power and coercive power, however, at least three characteristics point up their differences. First, the attitude of a child toward his parent is more favorable if the parent uses reward power. A second difference is that surveillance is more difficult with coercive power because the child is motivated to hide his behavior from the parent, whereas he wants to make the parent aware of his obedience if reward is the basis for influence. A third factor distinguishing between reward power and coercive power is that rewards may make a child *want* to comply more, thus increasing his perceived choice in the matter.

One rule states that the sooner the adult can reduce the use of power and control without sacrificing the quality of the child's behavior, the sooner the child will move toward maturity. Again, maturity involves acquiring more independence based on an internalized control system. As teachers move to less use of power and control techniques, often a *temporary* regression occurs in the quality of behavior. That is, when children move into an environment characterized by more freedom and less direction, they often behave less maturely. Examples of this immaturity are the behavior of children attending a summer camp and the behavior of high school graduates attending their first semester at a university.

For many of these students, this is their first emancipation from the supervision and control they have experienced in their family residence. Usually it takes a year for the adolescent to adjust to this new-found freedom. The observation is so frequent at almost all ages that it almost approaches a general law from kindergarten to the university. When new freedoms are encountered, they are frequently abused, and behavior regresses.

However, society is governed in such a way that such errors are usually temporary, and the resultant growth overshadows any temporary regression. Do not let this temporary loss of control deter you from developing a more maturity-producing control by using the following low-power techniques.

Recommended Teacher Approaches

This section is a summary and analysis of ways to use both low- and high-power child-rearing techniques.

Child Guidance Techniques

Low Power

1. Induction: logic that is other-oriented, empathy, sympathy, love.
2. Induction: logic that is self-oriented.
3. Natural consequences: self- and other-oriented.

Intermediate or Group Approaches

4. Mutual agreements and logical consequences.
5. Group- and leader-derived consequences, including social.
6. Approval withdrawal (not love withdrawal).

High Power

7. Love withdrawal.
8. Punish power.
9. Reward power.

The listing is hierarchal; however, considerations suggest that the ordering is tenuous.

First, one or more of these techniques could be used simultaneously, and an adult may vacillate between them. Also, they are not exclusive of one another, and the implementation of one technique might inadvertently elicit another.

Low-power techniques. Low-power techniques are primarily cognitive approaches. The teacher assists the child to perceive the effects of his action on other people and on himself. Even young children can understand that their actions can cause unpleasant experiences for others, and this knowledge is sufficient to inhibit antisocial behavior. Sensitivity in a young child can be discerned, such as when a parent intentionally engages in fake crying. The child will immediately show signs of his own distress and usually will try to stop the mother's crying. On the other hand, parental delight shown through laughter is contagious and is the motivating force for many friendly games between parents and children.

The psychologist most responsible for the development and identification of a technique based on the ability of the child to empathize and perceive some mental perspective of the feelings of others is Martin Hoffman at the University of Michigan. He points out that introduction to empathy largely involves giving explanations:

Examples are pointing out the physical requirements of the situation or the harmful consequences of the child's behavior for himself or others. These techniques are less punitive than power assertion or love withdrawal, and are more of an attempt to persuade or convince the child that he should change his behavior in the prescribed manner. Also included are techniques which appeal to conformity-inducing agents that already exist, or potentially exist, within the child. Examples are appeals to the child's pride, strivings for mastery and to be "grown up," and concern for others.

One type of induction, called Other-Oriented *induction, is singled out for special attention in this review because of our own research suggests its importance. The techniques used contain references to the implications of the child's behavior for another person. This may be done by directly pointing out or explaining the nature of the consequences (e.g. if you throw snow on their walk, they will have to clean it up all over again; pulling the leash like that can hurt the dog's neck; that hurts my feelings). This points out the relevant needs or desires of others (e.g. He's afraid of the dark, so please turn the light back on.) It also explains the motives underlying the other person's behavior toward the child (e.g., Don't yell at him, he was only trying to help). (Hoffman, 1970, p. 286.)*

165

In induction, the teacher helps the child understand reasons for engaging in appropriate behavior and for refraining from undesirable acts. The intent is to induce in the child conceptions and feelings. The teacher points out the consequences, material, logical, or emotional, of certain acts on either the child (self-oriented) or others (other-oriented) and attempts to show that acts have positive or negative consequences either for the child or for other people.

Such statements can produce either a cognitive understanding or an emotional state appropriate for the act being discussed. They need not always be negative. For example, the teacher may say, "Look at your friend now that you let her have your turn, see how happy she is." Or, "Don't you feel better now that you have cleaned your desk?" Nevertheless, many of the induction statements will elicit guilt or function as a reward or a punishment. Thus, they are not clearly separated from either love withdrawal or power assertion. Some situations do have elements of both. It is difficult to separate clearly the effects of withdrawing love in the form of rejecting or ignoring the child and indicating disappointment; both have elements of both love withdrawal and induction. Many teachers make it very clear that they are hurt or disappointed, but they may do so without saying that love and respect is being withdrawn from the child.

Generally, induction should include drawing generalizations from acts rather than focusing on a specific act. In addition, the induction method may occur in advance through discussion or vicarious experience. In a review of research indicating the relative comparative effectiveness of these methods, Hoffman (1970) indicates why, in his opinion, induction is clearly the most superior method of producing internalized behavior.

1. *They explain the consequences of the child's behavior, therefore directing the child's attention away from a personal evaluation and more toward an exact evaluation. Discipline becomes less dramatic because it is a concern with action rather than an evaluation or judgment of the child. An example of this distinction is "When you tease him or when you take away his toys, he will fight back" rather than "You started it."*
2. *Induction usually incorporates giving acts such as reparations or apologies, etc.*
3. *Most children are motivated to become more mature in the use of reasoning, and discussion induction helps the child to conceive that morality is a more mature or "grown up" behavior. It also communicates to the child that the parents see him as an individual capable of un-*

derstanding more mature concepts and with the ability to live up to a more mature set of standards.

4. Perhaps the most important aspect of the induction hinges on the development of a fundamental concept called empathy, which will be explained next. (Hoffman, 1970, p. 287.)

The proceeding advantages for the induction method of discipline rely upon a motivation or need to engage in approved social or moral action and to grow toward maturity. Note that this technique is based primarily on positive elements. The empathy concept adds another motivation to learn, involving the negative experiences that result when an individual has done something to another individual or group of individuals.

Applying Low-Power Techniques

To teach children self-control, resistance to temptation, and delay of gratification, parents and teachers might use the following techniques:

• *Be consistent* and follow through with promises so that the child will develop trust in adults.

• *Reward behavior that shows self-control.* Use statements such as the following: "You waited. Thank you. That shows you are growing up when you can wait so well."

"Thank you for letting Richard go first. You must be growing up when you can wait for your turn."

"I like the way you waited to eat your ice cream until everyone else had theirs, Kevin. I appreciate your good manners. You must be growing up when you can wait for the others."

"Since Richard is waiting so nicely for his turn, I am going to let him go first today."

• *Provide the child with numerous experiences to help him practice resistance to temptation.*

If a child is provided the proper environment, along with the absence of personal force and social and group coercion, the natural-consequences technique will be classified with *self-* and *other*-inductions. Here is a quotation from a leading proponent of the natural-consequences approach.

In some cases, however, it is necessary to contrive certain experiences. You can devise harmless means of showing the child that a stove is hot, that a needle pricks, or that a chair may fall over backward. Such facts are highly important; a casual method of calling them to the child's attention is far more impressive than intimidating him with wise, dire warnings. Likewise, you must see to it that certain consequences are invariably forthcoming. If the child is unpunctual at mealtimes, he should find that meals have already been served for all but him. If he fails to gather up his playthings, he ought not to be surprised if he is unable to find them the next day. If he is too slow in getting ready for walks and excursions, he could discover that you have gone off without him.

But the child must never consider these unpleasant effects of non-conformity as punishments or hostile moves on your part. On such occasions you must maintain a perfectly passive but benevolent attitude. You may express regret that the child has to go through these painful experiences, but in no event should you relieve him of them. (Dreikurs, 1972, p. 28.)

Ultimately, human beings must be self-directing rather than directed by others, and experiences during childhood determine the extent to which adult humans become especially self-directed in terms of desirable principles of conduct.

Intermediate or group approaches. The fourth, fifth, and sixth techniques are based on social influence. Included in these categories would be some of the techniques advocated by Dreikurs (1972). For example, under mutual agreements a teacher may agree to read a book to a class if the class agrees to be quiet during an instructional film. This may also apply to mutual agreements in terms of work-sharing and personal considerations.

Frequently, mutual agreements (as well as techniques five and six) require sanctions. Sanctions refer to negative consequences following the failure to keep an agreement, and sometimes refer to positive consequences following special arrangements. Note that overt material and social sanctions are not applied by the teacher in techniques seven, eight, and nine. Although it could be argued that there are subtle sanctions in techniques seven, eight, and nine, such assertions require some skillful use of logic and definitions. In techniques four, five, and six the use of sanctions is obvious and are often clearly defined. They are nevertheless distinguished from punishments by Dreikurs (1972):

One has already been discussed—namely, that consequences must have an inner logic understandable to the child. Telling him he cannot go to the movies if he does not eat his dinner has no logic; but if he does not come home from the movie on time, it is reasonable that he be told he may not go next week.

Consequences are a natural result of misbehavior—but they are not retaliations. If you say, "you have misbehaved, now you must . . ." that is punishment. Consequences are, rather an invitation: "As long as you misbehave, it will be impossible for you to . . ."

Another factor, distinguishing consequences from punishment, is the tone of your voice. If you speak in a harsh, angry voice then you punish. If you maintain a friendly attitude, you emphasize that it is the order which has to be observed, not your personal desire or your power. (Drei-kurs, pp. 30–31.)

Group- and leader-derived consequences include democratically derived rules and sanctions. When a legitimate and authorized leader of the group proposes rules or principles and concommitant consequences, it is considered democratic because the leader is essentially an extension of the group's wishes. Since the social rules in these cases are accepted democratically, they carry the same influence, weight, and justification as other democratically derived laws. This type of rule is the basis for much of our civic and social life as adults. Early acquaintance with mutual agreements is effective training for later participation in the social institutions of contemporary society.

Technique six, approval withdrawal, is also similar to that used by informal social groups. The informal social group may inform its member that his actions are unacceptable to the group, and while he is desired and loved, they cannot approve of his actions and thus must lower his status or even exclude him from the group. Sanctions can be used with a great amount of genuine concern and care for the individual even though he is ostracized and excluded. Teachers use this method by employing firm deliberate verbal statements to a child while simultaneously in manner and gesture assuring the child that he is still loved. In methods four, five, and six the group leader, teacher, principal, or mother and father need *not* use any *personal power.* They employ only power legitimately and overtly authorized by the group. Again, *no personal power* need be elicited to produce change, maintain order, or to guide behavior of another. In using personal power, the parent will likely be engaging techniques one, two, and three, which will now be discussed.

High-power techniques. These high-power techniques are based on the use of a number of controls given to socialization agents. Teachers and parents, by judiciously using these powers, can effect control over the behavior of children. However, the effectiveness of any of these high-power techniques (reward, punishment, and love withdrawal) is based on the premise that the socialization agent is able to maintain control over the important reinforcers of the child. However, control or power decreases each year until the child reaches adulthood.

NOTES

Boyce, W. B., & Jensen, L. *Moral Reasoning: A Philosophical—Psychological Integration.* Lincoln, Nebraska: University of Nebraska Press, 1978.

Dreikurs, R., & Soltz, V. *Children the Challenge.* New York: Hawthorn Books, 1964.

Erikson, E. H. *Children and Society.* New York: Norton, 1950.

Finett, H. *Between Parent and Child.* New York: Macmillan, 1965.

Gordon, T. *Parent Effectiveness Training: The No-lose Program for Raising Responsible Children.* New York: Wyden, 1970.

Hoffman, M. "Moral Development." In Mussen, P. (ed.) *Carmichael's Manual of Child Psychology.* New York: Wiley, 1970.

Kohlberg, L. Stage and Sequence: "The Cognitive Developmental Approach to Socialization." In Goslin, D. A. *Handbook of Socialization: Theory and Practices,* Chicago: Rand McNalley, 1971.

Leeper, M. R. "Dissonance, Self perception, and Honesty in Children." *Journal of Personality and Social Psychology.* (257), 1973, pp. 65–75.

Mazlow, A. *Maturation and Personality.* New York: Harper & Row, 1954.

Peck, P. F. & Havighurst, R. J. *The Psychology of Character Development.* New York: Wiley, 1962.

Pepitone, A., McCauley, C., & Hammond, P. "Change in Attractiveness of a Forbidden Toy as a Function of Severity of Threat," *Journal of Experimental Social Psychology.* (3), 1967, pp. 221–29.

Pinot, J. *The Moral Judgment of the Child.* New York: The Free Press, 1969.

Sundley, R. "Early Nineteenth Century American Literature on Child Rearing." In Evans, E. D. *Children: Readings in Behavior and Development.* New York: Holt, Rinehart, and Winston, 1968.

ABOUT THE AUTHORS

LARRY C. JENSEN is presently associated with two universities, as professor of psychology at Brigham Young University and as professor of family and human development at Utah State University. He has published articles in educational journals and has been author and coauthor of several books, including *Moral Reasoning* (University of Nebraska Press); *What's Right* (Public Affairs Press); *Feelings, That's Not Fair,* and *Influence: What It Is and How to Use It* (Brigham Young University Press).

KAREN M. HUGHSTON is program director of child care curriculum at New River Community College in Virginia. She has published in professional journals and has conducted workshops for parents. She is the mother of five.